America Accept the Truth, Repent, and Save Our Country

Drop the Hate and Communicate the Love of Christ

Dr. Derek Lawrence-Harper

Copyright © 2023 Dr. Derek Lawrence-Harper.

All rights reserved. No part of this book may be used or reproduced by any means, graphic, electronic, or mechanical, including photocopying, recording, taping or by any information storage retrieval system without the written permission of the author except in the case of brief quotations embodied in critical articles and reviews.

LifeRich Publishing is a registered trademark of The Reader's Digest Association, Inc.

LifeRich Publishing books may be ordered through booksellers or by contacting:

LifeRich Publishing
1663 Liberty Drive
Bloomington, IN 47403
www.liferichpublishing.com
844-686-9607

Because of the dynamic nature of the Internet, any web addresses or links contained in this book may have changed since publication and may no longer be valid. The views expressed in this work are solely those of the author and do not necessarily reflect the views of the publisher, and the publisher hereby disclaims any responsibility for them.

Any people depicted in stock imagery provided by Getty Images are models, and such images are being used for illustrative purposes only. Certain stock imagery © Getty Images.

Scripture taken from the King James Version of the Bible.

ISBN: 978-1-4897-4697-9 (sc)
ISBN: 978-1-4897-4699-3 (hc)
ISBN: 978-1-4897-4698-6 (e)

Library of Congress Control Number: 2023905542

Print information available on the last page.

LifeRich Publishing rev. date: 04/20/2023

Preface

America is the author's home, and he loves his country. The foundation of our country stated that we are one nation under God. However, America's application of biblical principles in America is a matter of dispute. Select information about America's history has been hidden, distorted, changed, and erased. The Pandemic of 2020 restricted our freedom and installed fear in some individuals. 2 Timothy 1:7 stated that God hath not given us the spirit of fear, but of power, and of love, and of a sound mind. If God did not give us the spirit of fear, we can assuredly know that it comes from the Devil/Satan/Lucifer through his demonic demon/angels. The bible stated that God has given us the spirit of power, of love, and of a sound mind however the devil seeks to steal our power, kill our love, and destroy our minds. Satan has infiltrated America in a multitude of areas. Henceforth, the author's challenge to everyone who reads this book to pray, ponder, research, and have an open mind because some of the contents of this book may challenge your traditional thinking and personal beliefs.

The American Civil Liberties Union (ACLU) reminds us that the First Amendment to the United States Constitution says that everyone in the U.S. has the right to practice his or her own religion, or no religion. The amendment was designed to guarantee separation of church and state to keep the government out of religion. However, churches who receive tax exempt status potentially allow the government at its discretion to place restrictions on a church's freedom of speech. Therefore, ministers, pastors, reverends, priests, bishops, apostles, rabbis, and any other title of religious authority's sermons may avoid controversial or political issues. Henceforth, the author will discuss issues that are often avoided in church sermons.

The author believes that the infiltration of the devil into the American churches has weakened the influence of the church. Satan targets church leaders tempting them to commit gross sin to damage the churches influence upon the community, reduce church membership, and keep the non-religious citizens from joining the church. Select churches chose to offset the negative damage to their religious institution's respect and reputation by accepting worldly perspectives and ignore things the bible clearly opposes. A church's survival needs membership, tithes, and donations from its members to pay bills and in wealthy churches to live in excess. The author is not attacking wealthy churches, but he is claiming that he believes some wealthy churches will avoid certain topics that may scare or turn members away. If what the author says is true about churches avoiding certain issues, that is a form of compromised Christianity. Unfortunately, America has a history of tunnel vision, meaning that certain people have limited perspectives by focusing on what they want and ignoring or disregarding other aspects.

God's timing is not our timing, but the bible is clear that judgment will come. America will be judged for its misdeeds one day. It is the author's hope that people will re-read the bible and encourage people to read this book to know that the author's goal is to first save souls and second save our country. Ideally, we need to be in a financial position to help others. To resolve problems in this country we must be honest and accept the truth to move forward. Most Americans including the author need all their income to pay bills and have means to enjoy themselves. The true minority in America is the rich who do not live paycheck to paycheck but have either generational wealth or maximized their talents to become prosperous. Hopefully, anyone who became rich did not compromise their morality or abuse, misuse, or oppress others for their personal gain. If so, pray that they repent. Our country is in trouble as Compromised Christianity, Atheism, Agnosticism, and Satanic influence is on the rise while Bible Believing Christians are declining, getting older, and are dying off. It has been said that those who ignore history repeat history. Dr. Martin Luther King once stated that truth suppressed to earth shall rise again. The author is here to talk about the truth that is rising in our time now. With the internet it is easy to search for information about different topics. We must use discernment to determine what is fact and what is fiction. Our great country has a history of suppressing truth to maintain a desired perception by those who benefit most from the desired perception. Every topic has an opposing viewpoint, and it is unlikely that everyone will have the same viewpoint. The author believes if our country will turn back to biblical roots per what the bible says, accept the truth, repent, forgive others, forgive self, reverse the curse, and follow the Lord we can save our great nation.

History has examples of great and powerful nations with a feared military such as the Greek Empire and Roman Empire who fell after complacency and immorality crept into their societies along with other factors. One of the most powerful foundations of the United States was its moral values. In the past individuals have been guilty of disregarding moral values taught by Christianity and the freedom of religion. In truth, the United States has an ugly history of prejudice, racism, and injustice. However, the United States also has a beautiful history especially during times of crisis to be helping neighbors, charitable, and compassionate. During times of crisis, I have seen people disregard the differences for the common good. If we as a country can show compassion during times of crisis, why not do it all the time because that is what God wants from us. Therefore, we need to first look towards the Lord for help and He will work through people and things that can be effective in the lives of believers. Insomuch, if we play the blame game, belittle the opposing side, speak hatred on others, or think politicians and money will fix our problems we need to recheck our history.

There are good and bad people in our country of all so-called races and ethnicities. The author believes that good people outweigh the bad and there is hope for our country to gain strength during turmoil. If bad people outweighed our good people in our country, we still have enough righteous people at this time for God to hear us. The bible teaches us that Sodom and Gomorrah were not destroyed because of their sin but because they did not have ten righteous people living there. The bible also teaches us that after the reluctant Jonah preached to the city of Nineveh that the people repented, and their city was not destroyed because of God's grace and mercy toward the people being willing to listen and change. Today, our cities represent a modern-day Nineveh as well as Sodom and Gomorrah because people openly sin against God but fortunately our cities have righteous bible believing Christians. Nevertheless, we have Christians that compromise the faith by accepting things that are contrary to what the bible states fulfilling the prophecy in 2 Timothy chapter 4 where people will flock to teachers who will overlook their sin, permit their lust, and lack teaching/preaching sound doctrine.

The focus of this book consists of leading people to Christ by first addressing unresolved issues in our country that are dismissed and ignored by the mainstream population. Leviticus 19:18 in the Old Testament as well as the books of Matthew, Mark, Luke, Romans, Galatians, and James each mentions how we are commanded to Love our neighbors as ourselves. None of the chapters says love your neighbors except if they are so-called black, so-called Jew, so-called Native American, or any other ethnicity or race. God wants us to love our neighbors as ourselves and from the author's observation people make exceptions to fit their personal viewpoint. The author makes a strong effort to live his life according to the standards of the bible contrary to how he used to live and tried to choose what he would follow and make the bible fit him. The author still is not perfect, but he is better than he used to be and improving each day regarding morality and spirituality. The author recognizes there are groups and classes of people in America who are not given the same level of respect. The bible tells us that God is not a respecter of persons therefore we should not be either. The author believes that if enough people accept the truth, repent, follow the Lord, reverse the curse, forgive others and themselves they can delay or save America from God's wrath and judgement. Do not fool yourself because the bible warns about the judgment of unrepented people. People do not repent because of their pride. Pride leads people to become addicted to being right, being first, and being superior. The author has seen ministries focus on other ministries to claim them false and make their ministry correct. The bible also tells us that pride comes before the fall and the United States has been a prideful nation for a long time. In the late 1960s Dr. Martin Luther King Jr. declared that America must repent of its deeds. Dr. King and Malcolm X. gathered information and were going to make demands upon the United States but both men were assassinated before that could happen and their plan was dissolved. However, the author believes that both men also uncovered truth about who were the indigenous people of America per historian Dane Calloway's video.

The United States gives honor to Christopher Columbus for discovering America but that was a lie because you cannot discover something where people already live. Our nation is increasing disrespectful behavior toward people, especially if their thoughts and beliefs are different from the majority group or power group. The highest position in America is the President of the United States who is verbally abused in the media and disrespected by people. Name calling, slander, false claims, and lies are commonplace. The author hates stereotyping people, labeling people, and disrespecting people. However, there are two groups of people, if someone determines hate speech towards those groups, a person could be fined, suspended, or lose their job and reputation. The author does not have a personal issue with either of the two groups because the author is against oppression, regression, or depression of any group of people. Henceforth, the bible says to love thy neighbor as thyself in the Old Testament in the Book of Leviticus therefore people who practice Judaism and Islam who accept the five books of Moses should practice loving each other as well as New Testament believing Christians.

There are a group of people in America who are disrespected, stereotyped, and labelled more than any other people and they fit the curses of Deuteronomy 28 better than any other people on the planet. Please note that the author has love for all ethnicities and so-called races of people on the earth because he truly tries to abide by love your neighbor as thyself. Therefore, he has no malice or hatred towards any group of people as he seeks to prove his belief of who the lost and scattered tribes of Israel and Judah are today.

Identifying the Historic Lost and Scattered Tribes of Israel and Judah to Unify Them with the Gospel of Jesus Christ is a bible study that aims to use the bible, apocryphal books, history, theories, myths, and not so commons sense to find the lost people. The author believes the lost and scattered tribes hidden in plain sight, however through propaganda and conspiracy has kept people disillusioned about true history. The author believes that individual people will find his research controversial and may object or be dismissive regarding his perspective and use of sources. However, bible prophecy is most essential element regarding identifying the lost and scattered tribes of Israel and Judah. Nevertheless, the most crucial factor upon identifying the lost is reconnecting them to covenants of their ancestors and grafting them back with God and planting the seeds to accept Jesus Christ as Lord and Savior.

There are people today trying to predict when our Lord and Savior Jesus Christ is going to return. More people are telling us that we are in the last days. The author will not predict when the Lord is returning because the bible tells us that not even the Son knows when He will be sent back for judging the nations. Forasmuch, when the author studied the bible and realized that men of God can negotiate with God such as Abraham did regards to Sodom and Gomorrah. The author also seen how enthusiastic God is about getting His will done as He spared Jonah who disobeyed him because God wanted the people of Nineveh to repent and be saved from judgement. Both the Old and New Testaments give examples of how God wants us to repent and change wrong ways to righteous behavior. The author is completely annoyed by so-called whites against so-called blacks and vice versa in America. Supremacy by any so-called race or ethnicity is wrong. Yet mankind periodically seems to have individuals seeking the power of superiority of others. In the United States the dominion of one so-called race over another is one sided and the contents of this book may be difficult for the privileged so-called race to digest. The author asked that all people read the information, research it, pray for it, and accept what they believe is true based upon information and not emotion. Insomuch, if Americans would judge people's behavior by the content of their character and not the color of their skin America would be genuinely great.

The author believes that America has the foundation to remain a powerful nation and become genuinely great. However, America must stop putting a bandage on its problems, self-medicating through substance abuse, and character assassinating those who speak against the wrongs of this country. The author is often annoyed when so-called white contributors are omitted from the struggles for freedom and equality in our country such as escaping slavery and the Civil Rights movement. The author is equally if not more annoyed when the church ignores the lack of value of human lives because the victim's skin tone is different from their own. The church needs to claim its powerful voice in America. God sent His Only Begotten son to save the entire world for those who will receive Him.

The information provided in the upcoming chapters may not align with most people's prior knowledge about the assorted topics including the author's prior perspectives. The author found the information uncomfortable until he began to pray, reflect, repent of past mindsets, forgive himself, forgive others who offended him, and focus on the instructions of the scriptures. Through diligent research and searching multiple sources were various conclusions drawn about what is mentioned in this book. The author asks that anyone who reads this book have an open mind and be ready to research the information for themselves. Please do not be quick to disregard everything if there are one or two aspects of this book with which you do not agree. America is too quick to dismiss what does not fit in its thinking. Pray, ponder the Word, fast if needed, and seek the Holy Spirit for validation of the information in this book.

Contents

Part 1: Bible Prophecy

Chapter 1   The Blessings of Obedience 1
Chapter 2   The Curses of Disobedience 7
Chapter 3   The Lost Tribes of Israel 25
Chapter 4   The Scattering of Judah 30

Part 2: Biblical Genealogy

Chapter 5   Connections to the Patriarchs 49
Chapter 6   The Two Nations of Jacob and Esau 56

Part 3: Identity

Chapter 7   Who is Who? 67

Part 4: Book of Mormon

Chapter 8   Overview of The Church of Jesus Christ
             of Latter-Day Saints 77
Chapter 9   Connection to Biblical Genealogy 86
Chapter 10 Book of Mormon Perceived References to
             Skin Color 92
Chapter 11 Carnal and Spiritual Interpretations 102

Part 5: The Author's Theology

Chapter 12 Overview of the Author's Theology 111

Part 6: Backlash

Chapter 13 Backlash From Bible Traditionalist 129
Chapter 14 Backlash From White Supremacist 132
Chapter 15 Backlash From Black Supremacists....................... 138
Chapter 16 Backlash From Major Media................................... 143
Chapter 17 Backlash From the Church of Jesus Christ
             of Latter-Day Saints.. 146

Part 7: Teaching the Gospel

Chapter 18 The Gospel of Jesus Christ..................................... 155
Chapter 19 How The Author's Theory Connects to
             the Gospel of Jesus Christ 159
Chapter 20 How to Teach the Gospel to the Lost and Scattered ... 164

Dedication:
To my wife: Dr. Jacqueline Lawrence-Harper
To whom is my daily reminder of what
serving the Lord looks like.

Part One
Bible Prophecy

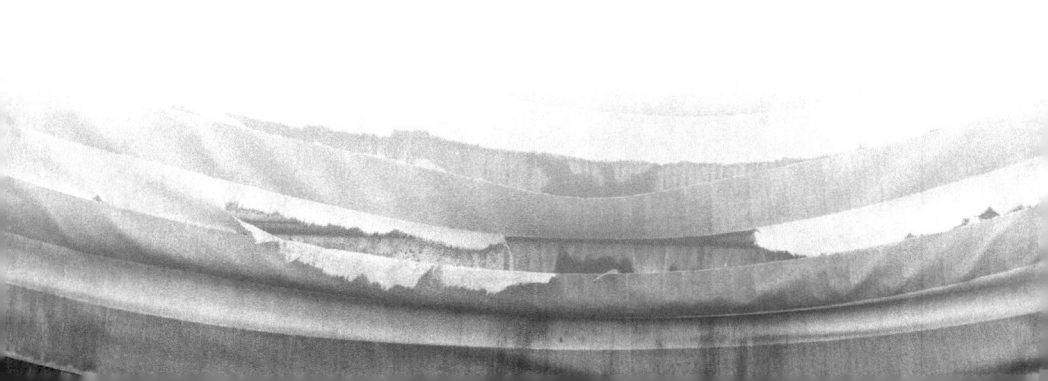

Chapter 1

The Blessings of Obedience

All faith-based people in the America and around the world would love to reap the blessings of God, but individual people are not willing to be obedient to His word. God will not accept mocking, and I do not believe that He likes being used as an ATM machine or a sugar daddy. [1] "Be not deceived; God is not mocked: for whatsoever a man soweth, that shall he also reap." Therefore, when we are obedient to God, we can receive blessings and when we are not obedient, we may receive consequences.

God made a covenant with the patriarch Abraham because of his obedience. When Abraham was ninety years old the Lord appeared to him while his name was Abram and told him to walk before him and be perfect. [2] "And I will make my covenant between me and thee and will multiply thee exceedingly." Therefore, we must be obedient to receive blessings and to multiply exceedingly. The exceeding blessings can be confusing to people because our flesh looks at blessings as prosperity. Henceforth, we need to delve into the topic of blessings verses to prosperity.

Prosperity is defined as wealth, money, possessions, status, and influence. Prosperity can be a blessing from God, but it can also be a gift from Satan. The devil was bold enough to tempt Jesus and took Him to an exceedingly high mountain to show Him all the

---

[1] Galatians 6:7 (KJV)
[2] Genesis 17:2 (KJV)

kingdoms of the world. ³ "And saith unto Him, all these things will I give thee, if thou wilt fall and worship me." Jesus refused the devil's offer and rebuked him by saying get the hence Satan and he left him alone. Therefore, not all gifts of prosperity come from God, and this can really confuse people.

How can we tell the difference between which blessings of prosperity come from God and which come from the devil? We must know the scriptures for ourselves and have a sense of right and wrong. For instance, in our times, we know that gangsters and drug dealers are not living for God because the way they acquire their wealth causes others to become addicted to substances, lose personal possessions, cause physical harm, or live-in fear. Unfortunately, we have individual preachers who are more like gangsters and spiritual drug dealers than men of God. ⁴ "Beware of false prophets, which come to you in sheep's clothing, but inwardly they are ravening wolves." This is a major issue because they claim to be representatives of God, but their hearts focus on what they can gain by using God for their personal prosperity. However, not all prosperous preacher, prophets, apostles, and those who say they are men of God are inwardly ravening wolves: some are sincere blessed men of God.

God does prosper individual men of God by blessing them. However, it becomes more confusing to those who have a desire to serve God to know who to listen to or follow. Individuals might think that small congregations lack God's presence which is usually incorrect. Some people assume that large, wealthy churches receive God's blessings. Therefore, how can we tell who is a true man of God? We must know the Bible and listen carefully to multiple messages. Men of God should be uplifting but occasionally they should teach their followers to confront their personal worldly desires or own their poor choices and mistakes. ⁵ "For the time will come when they will not endure sound doctrine; but after their own lusts shall they heap

---

³ Matthew 4:9 (KJV)

⁴ Matthew 7:15 (KJV)

⁵ 2 Timothy 4:3 (KJV)

to themselves teachers, having itching ears." [6] "and they shall turn away their ears from the truth and shall turn unto fables." People love to hear that God will bless them if they just believe and are not challenged to change anything. Some people become angry if you say something about them that they do not want to hear. Individuals, if not most people, are spiritually immature and cannot manage the truth. [7] "And I, brethren, could not speak unto you as unto spiritual, but as unto carnal, even as unto babes in Christ." Therefore, people who are new to the gospel of Christ need time to mature in the Word and cannot partake of the heavier levels of truth.

A major blow to the community of believers in Christ occurred when individual pastors and men of God were exposed and found guilty of worldly crimes such as solicitation of prostitutes, adultery, homosexuality, extortion, drugs and alcohol use, and lying to the people. These crimes painted a bad image of men of God, and their images became ingrained in individual people's minds making people reluctant to trust preachers. They believe that preachers require tithes, offerings, and seeds so they can obtain wealth and call themselves blessed. In our minds, negative images and beliefs have longer lasting effects than positive images. The preconceived beliefs of individual people make it impossible to reach them. However, there is another side to the prosperous pastor's congregation.

There are congregations that will ignore anything the religious leader does because they love him so much. Without people realizing it they make their pastor a god. They will give their pastor anything he asks for without hesitation and become angry with anyone who challenges what is going on in the church. They want their pastor to look good and blessed. Another thing that happens is a congregation will think they are the **only true church**, and they are the chosen of God. That means that they are the only ones who are right about God and everyone else is wrong or is of the devil. Furthermore, they think that they are the exception because God chose them, and

---

[6] 2 Timothy 4:4 (KJV)

[7] 1 Corinthians 3:1 (KJV)

they are privileged to do whatever they want because of their status with God.

The lost and scattered tribes of Israel and Judah became comfortable with their status with God and began to act like they world. The behaviors and attitudes of the tribes of Israel and Judah caused them to disregard the covenant God made with their Patriarch Abraham, this led them into captivity. God took away His hedge of protection over them and allowed them to fight for themselves which did not have a favorable result for the tribes of Israel and Judah. God made it known to Abraham after he received the promise and blessings what would happen to his descendants. [8] "And he said unto Abram, know of a surety that thy seed shall be a stranger in a land that is not theirs, and shall serve them; and they shall afflict them four hundred years." This referred to slavery that occurred in Egypt after the Pharoah during that period no longer valued Joseph's contribution. During the time before God's chosen people suffered enslavement, they were growing strong and multiplying faster than the Egyptians. However, Abraham received information that after four hundred years that the nation that ruled over them would receive judgment. [9] "And, that nation, whom they shall serve, will I judge and afterward shall they come out with great substance." Therefore, after they became humble, they received blessings with great substance.

God revealed His blessings and curses of obedience to Moses in Deuteronomy. In the first verse of Deuteronomy 28. God gave the people of Israel a conditional blessing for their potential obedience. [10] "And it shall come to pass, if thou shalt hearken diligently unto the voice of the LORD thy God, to observe and to do all his commandments which I command thee this day, that the LORD thy God will set thee on high above all nations of the earth: In the next eleven verses, God tells them what blessings they would receive, which included His protection from other nations, an endless supply of food and goods, health, wealth, treasures, and finances that would allow them to

---

[8] Genesis 15:13 (KJV)
[9] Genesis 15:14 (KJV)
[10] Deuteronomy 28:1 (KJV)

lend and not borrow." In Deuteronomy 13, God reminds Israel of the conditions of the blessing. [11] "And the LORD shall make thee the head, and not the tail; and thou shalt be above only, and thou shalt not be beneath; if that thou hearken unto the commandments of the LORD thy God, which I command thee this day, to observe and to do them:" Therefore, the people of Israel were intended to be the leading nation on earth and not behind or below any nation.

God, through the prophet Moses, informed Israel of the blessings they could obtain through obedience, but He also gave the people a command and stern warning. He told them not to detour from His Word in any direction or go worship other gods. [12] "But it shall come to pass, if thou wilt not hearken unto the voice of the LORD thy God, to observe to do all his commandments and his statutes which I command thee this day; that all these curses shall come upon thee and overtake thee." We know that the Bible tells us that the children of Israel as a whole did not obey the voice of the Lord and did break the commands that were given them thus, they lost their land. Nevertheless, God is faithful and is not on the same timetable that we are on.

God did not forget the covenant that He made with Abraham. [13] "That in blessing I will bless thee, and in multiplying I will multiply thy seed as the stars of the heaven, and as the sand which is upon the seashore; and thy seed shall possess the gate of his enemies." [14] "And in thy seed shall all the nations of the earth receive blessings, because thou hast obeyed my voice." The number of stars in heaven and the sands upon the seashore is uncountable, humans cannot comprehend the amount. This could be the first indication that all people on earth, because of Abraham, could receive blessings on earth because of their biological connections to him. The promise to Abraham made after he assessed if he would sacrifice Isaac. When God saw Abraham would hold nothing back, he blessed Abraham and all his future seed. However, the future blessings would have stipulations.

---

[11] Deuteronomy 28:13 (KJV)
[12] Deuteronomy 28:15 (KJV)
[13] Genesis 22:17 (KJV)
[14] Genesis 22: 18 (KJV)

Abraham received notification that his offspring would go into captivity. Abraham also received notification of the blessings they could receive. [15] "Behold, I set before you this day a blessing and a curse." [16] "A blessing, if ye obey the commandments of the LORD your God, which I command you this day: Human choices of the carnal flesh kept Israel from receiving God's best for them." Instead, they brought a curse upon them, and individuals still suffer from this day. However, it is also possible for individuals to receive the blessings of God by grace and a sincere effort to do that which is right. The bible mentions more about the struggles of Israel and Judah through their disobedience that their obedience, but the bible provides good news through the savior and redeemer Jesus Christ. It was impossible for the Israelites and Judah to keep all the law in their flesh, so God already had a plan for a redeemer. Fortunately, the bible has individual stories of how a person can receive salvation from their sins by accepting, believing, and proclaiming that Jesus Christ is their Lord and Savior.

The New Testament highlights what life with Christ can be like. When we accept the grace of God and seek our holy purpose in this world we learn how to grow in obedience to the word of God. [17] "Who hath saved us, and called us with a holy calling, not according to our works, but according to his own purpose and grace, which gave us in Christ Jesus before the world began, the love, grace, and mercy of God helps us to be obedient to His Word by creating a sincere desire to serve Him." Also, the ability and desire to repent for our sins can cleanse us from the guilt of our errors. God wants His covenant people of the lost and scattered tribes of Israel and Judah to accept this gift and receive their inheritance. Jesus' sacrifice and salvation is for all people who accept Him. Henceforth, if faith-based people in America repent for their mistakes poor choices and obey God's Word the country can be saved.

---

[15] Exodus 11:26 (KJV)
[16] Exodus 11:27 (KJV)
[17] 2 Timothy 1:9 (KJV)

Chapter 2
The Curses of Disobedience

The children of Israel and Judah suffered the curses of disobedience according to the scriptures. They broke the covenant with the "Most High God" and suffered the consequences for all the world to see. This book will examine the curses mentioned in the bible beginning with Deuteronomy Chapter 28. Therefore, upon the author reading the curses of this Deuteronomy Chapter 28, he believes it best describes one demographic group of people on earth today.

Deuteronomy Chapter 28 verse fifteen stated that if the Israelites did not hearken to the voice of the Lord and do what He said that the people would suffer for their disobedience. [18] "Cursed shalt thou be in the city, and cursed shalt thou be in the field." Some demographics of people have lived in the ghettos of major cities in America and across the world, but only one demographics suffered living in the ghettos and experienced slavery. [19] "Cursed shall be thy basket and thy store." According to the author who worked in management and stocking food for a couple of America's top food chains his opinions are the following. The quality of food in stores in is edible and can be prepared to taste great in American ghettos and rural areas. However, the quality of meat, produce, and healthy foods offerings are below the standards of food stores in the suburbs or affluent

---

[18] Deuteronomy 28:16 (KJV)
[19] Deuteronomy 28:17 (KJV)

neighborhoods. [20] "Cursed shall be the fruit of thy body, and the fruit of thy land, the increase of thy kine, and the flocks of thy sheep." According to various medical research studies individual experts believe that individual illnesses pass genetically to the next generation. The descendants of the Israelites may have generational curses in their families such as hypertension, heart disease, diabetes, as well as other ailments that are common to other demographics but may be higher in percentage than other demographics. Regarding those cursed in the land those enslaved upon release given opportunities to be sharecroppers, obtain farmland taken from them, and other tactics that resulted in losing their property. [21] "Cursed shalt thou be when thou comest in, and cursed shalt thou be when thou goest out." Very few demographics experienced living in fear of receiving beatings or killed without committing a crime. In the United States of America one demographic has suffered like an animal, sold, raped without consequence to the perpetrator, beaten without consequence to the perpetrator, lynched without consequence to the perpetrator, or killed in any manner without consequence to the perpetrator. Henceforth, upon reading the four previous courses, it begins to narrow down the possibilities to one demographic. Insomuch, if a person believes in biblical prophecy more than common perceptions and standard norms of thinking yet there is much more evidence in the upcoming verses to consider if the perception of one demographic is correct.

For the sake of time this book will hand pick certain verses that describe a certain demographic, and the curse of disobedience described in Deuteronomy Chapter 28. [22] "Thy sons and thy daughters shall be given unto another people, and thine eyes shall look, and fail with longing for them all day long; and there shall be no might in thine hand." In the days of slavery in the United States children were taken from their parents whenever the master seen fit. Today Child Protective Services takes children from parents of all races,

---

[20] Deuteronomy 28:18 (KJV)

[21] Deuteronomy 28:19 (KJV)

[22] Deuteronomy 28:32 (KJV)

but one demographic has their children taken more disproportionate than others. [23] "The Lord shall bring a nation against thee from far, from the end of the earth, as swift as the eagle flieth; a nation whose tongue thou shalt not understand." America is the only nation that is at the other end of the earth from the original location whose symbol is the eagle from the Israelites dispersed from Israel and Judah to the north of Assyria, Europe, Far East, and most impactfully Africa. During the Trans-Atlantic Slave trade people were taken from their land of origin to a world they could not understand the speech. [24] "And the Lord shall scatter thee among all people, from the one end of the earth even unto the other; and there thou shalt serve other gods, which neither thou nor thy fathers have known, even wood and stone." One demographic of people can be found on every continent but select people are disregarded and disrespected. The love of paper money which is made from the wood of trees and precious stones such as diamonds and rubies are valued, worshiped, and idolized today. Individual people of all races idolized the modern version of gods of money and jewelry. [25] "And the Lord shall bring thee into Egypt again with ships, whereof I spoke unto thee, thou shalt see it no more again: and there ye shall be sold unto your enemies for bondmen and bondwomen, and no man shall buy you." The United States of America is considered by individuals as the modern Egypt based upon select factors such as the pyramid on the back of the dollar bill, the pagan symbolism in the design of Washington D.C., small replica pyramids in places as Nevada, and Memphis Tennessee. Memphis Tennessee is also symbolic of Memphis Egypt which was located by Africa's longest river the Nile and Memphis Tennessee is locate by America's longest river the Mississippi. The previously mentioned could be coincidences, but the author wants to consider another fact. Since Jesus Christ died for our sins and paid the price for all people who accept him as Lord and Savior. Christians are free from the bondage of sin because of Jesus Christ. Deuteronomy

---

[23] Deuteronomy 28:49 (KJV)
[24] Deuteronomy 28:64 (KJV)
[25] Deuteronomy 28:68 (KJV)

28:68 stated that they will return to Egypt on ships and sold to their enemies as bondmen and bondwomen which are slaves. If America is symbolic for modern day Egypt, then only one demographic of people on earth fit the curses of Deuteronomy's verses. People purchased slaves for their usage but, nobody purchased the freedom of the people who came off the ships and they were sold into slavery from auction blocks to the highest bidder.

Servitude and slavery were a direct result of disobedience to God's word by the Israelites. God wanted to bless his children, but they were disobedient, and they received a consequence. However, God delights in blessing His people and gave the Israelites hope after receiving a consequence for disobedience. [26] "And shalt return unto the LORD thy God, and shalt obey his voice according to all that I command thee this day, thou and thy children, with all thine heart, and with all thy soul." [27] "That then the LORD thy God will turn thy captivity, and have compassion upon thee, and will return and gather thee from all the nations, whither the LORD thy God hath scattered thee." Insomuch, the Lord God always left room for repentance and re-establishment.

Various prophets in the bible spoke about future enslavement of the Israelites. Two of the major prophets Isaiah and Jeremiah prophesied about Israel's disobedience and future captivity beginning with Babylonia. Chapter 52 in the Book of Isaiah refers to Israelites being detached and asleep from a relationship with God in which they are told to wake up and become whom they were meant to be. [28] "Shake thyself from the dust; arise, and sit down, O Jerusalem: loose thyself from the bands of thy neck, O captive daughter of Zion." [29] "For thus saith the LORD, Ye have sold yourselves for naught; and ye shall be redeemed without money." The previous two verses seem like a reminder or continuation of the conditions of the curses from Deuteronomy Chapter 28: However, in Isaiah 52:3 states that they

---

[26] Deuteronomy 30:2 (KJV)
[27] Deuteronomy 30:3 (KJV)
[28] Isaiah 52:2 (KJV)
[29] Isaiah 52:3 (KJV)

will be redeemed without money which means the will be saved by a future Christ. Ironically, The Book of Isaiah is the same book that prophesies the birth of Christ in Chapter 7. The Book of Isaiah also spoke of the fall of Lucifer in 14:12 which the author brings up to make a point about the validity of the prophecies and claims in the Book of Isaiah. Therefore, it should be noted that God already had a plan for a savior in the Old Testament to overcome the fall of man through sin and disobedience along with combating the efforts of Lucifer to destroy God's people.

There is evidence that God does not curse people directly, but the choices people make open the door to be cursed. God is the master delegator because He communicates with us through angels, dreams, visions, people, and inspiration of The Holy Spirit. Likewise, when people open the door to curses the Lord allows Satan/Lucifer/The Devil and his demon angels to mess with our circumstances. One example was in the Book of Job when the Lord and Satan had a conversation about Job. Satan entered heaven with the sons of God (angels) in Job 1:6. [30] "And the LORD said unto Satan, whence comest thou? Then Satan answered the LORD, and said, from going to and from in the earth, and from walking up and down in it." The Lord began to rave about the dedication of Job to Satan and Satan challenged the Lord and said that Job was only dedicated because of the hedge of protection that God was providing him. [31] "Hast not thou made a hedge about him, and about his house, and about all that he hath on every side? thou hast blessed the work of his hands, and his substance is increased in the land." When the Lord lifted the protection from Job, Satan was able to mess with Job's circumstances which he hoped to turn Job against God. Likewise, the Israelites and Judah used to have a hedge of protection from the Lord but when they became disobedient their hedge of protection was removed and Satan was allowed to mess with their circumstances and cause misery and pain.

---

[30] Job 1:7 (KJV)
[31] Job 1:10 (KJV)

God is a merciful God, and He loves His people. However, God is also a God of order, commitment, and justice. When Israel and Judah began to serve other gods, they were out of order and broke their commitment to God. When that happened God was forced to inflict justice upon them. Justice served by God is not the same justice as man upon man because God does not live in our time. [32] "But, beloved, be not ignorant of this one thing, that one day is with the Lord as a thousand years, and a thousand years as one day." The Lord removes the hedge of protection from his people because their actions justified the allowance of Satan to cause havoc in their lives through oppressive people. Therefore, if justice is servitude, then multiple generations could be spent in slavery because of disobedience and non-repentance.

Unfortunately, individual people who become in power and take captives think they are gods and should be worshipped. [33] "Now these are the words of the letter that Jeremiah the prophet sent from Jerusalem unto the residue of the elders which were carried away captives, and to the priests, and to the prophets, and to all the people whom Nebuchadnezzar had carried away captive from Jerusalem to Babylon." Nebuchadnezzar thought that he should be worshipped and commissioned a statue of himself for the people to bow down to. [34] "Therefore, at that time, when all the people heard the cornet, flute, harp, sackbut, psaltery, and all kinds of music, all the people, the nations, and the languages, fell and worshipped the golden image that Nebuchadnezzar the king had set up." However, there were still individual faith filled Israelites among the captives of Judah and Israel who refused to worship other gods. [35] "Then was Nebuchadnezzar full of fury, and the form of his visage was changed against Shadrach, Meshach, and Abednego: therefore, he spoke, and commanded that they should heat the furnace one seven times more than it was wont to be heated." Shadrach, Meshach, and Abednego were thrown

---

[32] 2 Peter 3:8 (KJV)
[33] Jeremiah 29:1 (KJV)
[34] Daniel 3:7 (KJV)
[35] Daniel 3:19 (KJV)

into the fire for disobeying a worldly king but since they honored their spiritual king they were protected from the flames of the fiery furnace. [36] "Then Nebuchadnezzar spoke, and said, Blessed be the God of Shadrach, Meshach, and Abednego, who hath sent his angel, and delivered his servants that trusted in him, and have changed the king's word, and yielded their bodies, that they might not serve nor worship any god, except their own God." The king was astonished and was forced to recognize Israel and Judah's God as the real God. However, he still did not let the people go.

The Prophet Daniel had visions, but one included that his people would be able to return to Jerusalem. He was still in captivity when Babylon was taken over by Persia. During the reign of Cyrus, the King of Persia Daniel gained favor as he did before with Nebuchadnezzar when he interpreted his dream in Daniel Chapter 2. However, this time Israel and Judah were allowed to return to their country.

After the return Judah and Israel would turn from the Lord again and dispersed again. The Persian warriors defeated by the Greek warriors and Alexander the Great. During this time, the Greeks not only conquered Persia which is modern day all Turkey, Syria, Israel, Jordan, Iraq, Iran, Afghanistan, Pakistan, and small parts of bordering countries. He also conquered a great portion of Egypt in which he raided their archives and their gods. He defeated Persia around 334 B.C. to his death in 323 B.C. The kingdom was divided after his death until the Roman Empire took over in 27 B.C. to 476 A.D. The Romans were in control of the region during the birth and death of our Lord and Savior Jesus Christ from approximately 3 or 4 B.C. to 30 A.D. The Israelites were not slaves as we have learned slavery, but they were under the oppression of the Romans. When the Romans conquered Greece, they took what the Grecians took from Egypt to claim as their own gods. Ironically, the Egyptian, Greek, and Roman gods all have similar roles but different names.

In 70 A.D. the Jews we at war with the Romans and lost and were scattered and dispersed to after reigning for 4 years by Titus.

---

[36] Daniel 3:28 (KJV)

Individual Jews did return after that but were finally scattered and dispersed in 135 A.D. after the Romans were driven out by Simon Bar- Cochba in 132A.D. The Romans destroyed all evidence of Jews ever living in Jerusalem. The reign of Nebuchadnezzar began around 586 B.C. when they destroyed Solomon's Temple and the lost and scattered tribes of Israel dispersed to the north of Babylon and far south as Africa. In 70 A.D. and 135 A.D. a substantial number who were not enslaved escaped into Africa. Nevertheless, there seems to be a disconnect between the biblical Jews and modern-day Jews.

In 1917 Britain's Foreign Secretary Balfour declared conditional support for a homeland for the Jews in Palestine. In the 1930s Adolf Hitler begins with policy against the Jews in Germany and Eastern European countries which eventually develops into execution of Jewish people starting in 1938. The next year 1939 began World War II which Nazi Germany was attempting to take over Europe and the world. The Jews between 1939 and 1945 experience inhumane treatment including illegal experimentation, gas chambers, and mass graves during what is known as the Holocaust. The war ended in 1945 and in 1947 the United Nations approved the Jewish and Arab state of Palestine mandated by the British. In 1948 Israel declares itself as an independent Jewish state which was approved of by the United Nations. War in Palestine begins the next day between Israel and Arabs. Less than a year later 250, 000 Holocaust survivors relocate to Israel along with thousands of Yemen Jews. This is what we know about the lineage of modern Jews who are mostly known as Ashkenazi Jews. There have been individual wars with modern day Israel and today Israel is one of the countries with nuclear weapons better known as weapons of mass construction. Ironically, the disconnect the author speaks about has to do with war and peace.

The bible prophesies about how things will be when Israel and Judah return. Judah and Israel will be scattered through the corners of the earth and will be gathered up during a time of peace. [37] "And he shall judge among the nations and shall rebuke select people: and

---

[37] Isaiah 2:4 (KJV)

they shall beat their swords into plowshares, and their spears into pruninghooks: nation shall not lift sword against nation, neither shall they learn war anymore." The Book of Micah makes the same claim. [38] "And he shall judge among individual people, and rebuke strong nations afar off; and they shall beat their swords into plowshares, and their spears into pruninghooks: nation shall not lift a sword against nation, neither shall they learn war anymore." Chapter 11 in the Book of Isaiah explains how things should be when Israel and Judah are gathered, and peace will reign upon the earth. The author is not saying that today's Jews are not Jews because anyone who converts to a religion is recognized as one who is born into a religion. Furthermore, if a person is born into a country such as Israel, then they are an Israeli. It is documented that Ashkenazi Jews are Jews based upon their mother's lineage which is plausible and making them Semitic. In times of war and slavery men take the women of whom they conquered and bare children. The bible's genealogy for Jews from the tribe of Judah is based upon the father's lineage which was cut off between Nebuchadnezzar reign to the days of Roman dominion and after. Nevertheless, the conditions upon which modern Israel was given to the current Jews who are recognized is man made by the United Nations and Britain and not biblical prophecy or else there would be peace and return of the Messiah as king of kings and Lord of Lords as stated in chapter 1 in the Book of Revelations.

The current state of Israel should be honored and respected because Lord allowed this to happen or ordained it whether it is for a season or a long time. The author looks to the bible and is reminded of the story of King Saul and David. David was anointed as king prior to becoming king during Saul's reign. David served Saul and never disrespected Saul while he was king. Even when Saul tried to kill David, he continued to honor his position as king because the Lord allowed him to be king. When David had the opportunity to kill Saul, he did not but he let Saul know that he could have killed

---

[38] Micah 4:3 (KJV)

him. David waited for the Lord to remove Saul from his throne and then he was willing to fulfill his destiny as the King of Israel and Judah. The people of Israel and Judah wanted to be like other nations and demanded to have a king. The prophet Samuel with the Lords blessing anointed Saul as king. The throne of Israel was manufactured, but this was not God's best for Israel. When Saul became worldly and disobedient to God then a replacement in David was activated. The talents and skills of David was obvious to all, and he received more praises than Saul and he became jealous of David. Insomuch, Saul made sure that he stayed on top of David and kept him close and looked for the best opportunity to eliminate him.

Seventy-four percent of the people living in Israel claim to practice Judaism. Today the people in Israel enjoy the benefits of their status as Jews. Unfortunately, individual family members from the late 1930s and mid 1940s had to endure the horrors of the Holocaust. However, as awful as the Holocaust was it does not mirror the description of the curses of Deuteronomy 28. [39] "He shall lend to thee, and thou shalt not lend to him: he shall be the head, and thou shalt be the tail." Today select Jewish people are the lenders and own various banks. You can find individual Jewish leaders in respected professions in various nations. However, there is one demographic of people who are consistently the tail in every nation today. There are individual exceptions especially in entertainment, athletics, along with various professional fields but at a much smaller rate than other demographics.

It should be noted as the author has referred to one demographic as being the bloodline people of Israel or Judah that it is highly unlikely that anyone has a bloodline that is not a mixture of others. Even our Lord and Savior has a bloodline mixed with Canaanites, Moabites, a harlot, and others that we may not be sure of as mentioned in Matthew Chapter 1. However, it is difficult to overlook the people who best describe the curses of Deuteronomy 28. Nevertheless, the so-called African Americans should not become prideful with the

---

[39] Deuteronomy 28: 44 (KJV)

knowledge that the bible is referring to them because it means they were foolish enough to be God's chosen people and broke their end of the covenant. Furthermore, they refused accept Jesus Christ as their Lord and Savior while He was on the earth which individuals chose Barabbas.

In select ways so-called African Americans are still choosing Barabbas over Christ. Barabbas symbolizes danger, excitement, and fun while Christ represents love, purity, and peace which can be perceived as boring. In the Book of Matthew Chapter 27 Pilate declared himself innocent of Jesus blood and washed his hands but the people in the crowd said may the blood of Jesus be on us and our children. The author believes what happened to so-called African Americans is a manifestation of choosing Barabbas over Jesus for crucifixion. Fortunately, not all so-called African Americans desire Barabbas over Jesus. Nevertheless, so-called African Americans need to lift their heads and recognize that they are not inferior to any group of people but accept that they were humbled to realize that they are not superior either.

Racial superiority is a man-made creation which the gentiles need to be careful not to fall into the same pitfalls of the early Jews. The apostle Paul got fed up with preaching the gospel of Jesus Christ to the Jews. [40] "Then Paul and Barnabas waxed bold, and said, it was necessary that the word of God should first have been spoken to you: but seeing ye put it from you, and judge yourselves unworthy of everlasting life, lo, we turn to the Gentiles." Paul preached Christ to the gentiles, and they accepted the word of God and eventually spread the gospel throughout the world. The gentile nations were prospered by accepting and following the gospel. The Book of Genesis lists the genealogy of the sons of Noah in chapter 10. The gentiles are only mentioned among the lineage of Japheth in the bible even though individual people were taught that anybody who is a non-Jew is a gentile. [41] "By these were the isles of the Gentiles

---
[40] Acts 13:46 (KJV)
[41] Genesis 10:5 (KJV)

divided in their lands; everyone after his tongue, after their families, in their nations." Upon looking at a map today there are individual small and medium sized islands in the Mediterranean Sea in Europe by Greece and Italy. Insomuch, The Book of Jubilees states that the land of the north which is modern day Europe was appointed to the sons of Japheth.

Upon researching Genesis Chapter 9 which the patriarch Noah appointed blessings and curses the author noticed something peculiar in the King James Version that differs from individual modern versions of the bible. [42] "Noah said blessed be the Lord God of Shem and Canaan shall be his servant." Noah did not bless Shem he blessed the Lord God of Shem whom in the other books of the bible the line of Shem followed. He did not say that he blessed Shem like select newer versions state. The author found this to be significant because the line of Shem has suffered for their disobedience including being in servitude and slavery. Genesis Chapter 9 also had Noah making a statement about the Japheth that is peculiar and often overlooked. [43] "God shall enlarge Japheth, and he shall dwell in the tents of Shem; and Canaan shall be his servant." Noah did not bless Japheth but prophesied that he would be enlarged and dwell in the tents of Shem. Select modern versions have Japheth as being blessed and enslaving Canaan. However, we know from reading the bible that the promise land of Shem's line was called the land of Canaan. This shows that Canaan's line refused to volunteer for servitude and took a land that belonged to Shem. We know that the land belonged to Shem according to the Book of Jubilees which stated which land belonged to whom and said that Noah cursed anyone who took a land that was not allotted to them. Therefore, the curse of Canaan was about land ownership and not about Ham's seeing the nakedness of his father Noah while he was drunk.

The question remains why Japheth being enlarged and dwelling in the tents of Shem is not a blessing. Notice that the bible did not

---

[42] Genesis 9:26 (KJV)
[43] Genesis 9:27 (KJV)

describe how Japheth became enlarged or how they dwelt in the tents of Shem. History shows how individual members of the line of Japheth would colonize countries and set the countries up so they could rule, dominate, and take their resources without compensation. Select people of the European nations decided to interpret Noah cursing Canaan as an excuse to put darker skinned people in slavery. The Book of Jubilees stated that the lands to south known in modern days as the continent of Africa was given to Ham and his sons. Ham and his sons are widely accepted as the darker skinned people of the world by biblical scholars. However, there are a couple of problems with this logic. First Ham had three other sons who were not cursed by Noah and had nothing to do with anything. Second Canaan took the land which is modern day Middle East and not in Africa. It is reasonable to assume that individual Canaanites may have migrated to Africa as spouses to Hamites but primarily resided in the Middle East. Therefore, technically speaking Europeans should have gone to the Middle East to seek out the sons of Canaan for enslavement and not Hams' other three sons of Cush, Mizraim, or Phut. Furthermore, the cruelty of the enslavement by Europeans of Africans especially in America was not biblical. Slaves and servants were to be treated as human beings with rights and not as property such as cattle. In 1967 Martin Luther King Jr. said that America needed to repent from their immoral ways. Also, in 1967 Martin Luther King stated that Blacks should receive reparations which may have been in reference to his 1963 "I have a dream speech" which is overlooked reference to select blacks being indigenous to this land.

This book will expound upon the curses in detail however it must be examined how a different curse has led for people to believe that only a certain group of people is under a curse and how the scripture has been misused throughout the years to justify slavery. The latter part of Chapter Two will discuss Deuteronomy Chapter 28 and the conquering by King Nebuchadnezzar over Israel and Judah. However, the author would like to discuss the curse by Noah to Canaan, the son of Ham and explain why this has been troubling to him. The Israelites and the Egyptians offspring off Ham often interacted in the bible and the Israelites have been mistaken as Egyptians with Joseph, Moses, and the hiding of Jesus. The Israelites have spent multiple years in slavery as the sons of Shem but because of a curse upon one son of Ham. Insomuch, excerpts duplicated from a different book by the same author called "The Origins of SelFLESHNESS" to expound upon the perception of curses and slavery.

The most famous misstatements are the "Curse of Ham." Noah never cursed Ham, and he could not curse him after God blessed Noah and his three sons in Genesis Chapter 9. [44] "One of my most troubling areas in the bible consist of why Noah got angry at his son Ham because he seen his nakedness but instead of cursing Ham, he cursed Ham's son Canaan which is also Noah's grandson." The first thought is to take the bible at face value which is Noah felt disrespected by his son Ham. However, Noah feeling disrespected would not explain why Noah cursed Canaan. Individuals believe that Ham had sex with Noah's wife which would also be Ham's mother and had Canaan because of incest. This theory is based upon which states: [45] "The nakedness of thy father's wife shalt thou do not uncover it is thy father's nakedness." Even though I understand the rationale I still find this theory unlikely for a variety of reasons. First Ham had a wife and he had four sons by her and there was no need to be so desperate to sleep with or rape your own mother. Secondly, Ham's mom would not be so weak to have sex with her youngest son especially with her husband being alive. Third, Ham had to older brothers who would have caused Ham physical harm up to killing him for sleeping with their mother. Lastly, there are various theories to demonize Ham since he is believed to be the father of African nations to justify slavery.

Individual people still refer to the incident as the curse of Ham even though the bible clearly states Canaan was cursed. Worse, is the tale that individual people believe that Ham raped and sodomized his father Noah. Another story has Ham castrating his father so he

---

[44] The Origins of SelFLESHness Lawrence-Harper, Derek.
[45] Leviticus 18:8 (KJV)

would not be able to have more children so he would not have to split his inheritance of the earth with more siblings. I believe the above demonization of Ham was ridiculous and unmerited. I also do not believe that Ham merely seeing his father naked was enough to make Noah that angry. We must use common sense and realize that people regardless of the period are the same and no parent would get that angry over their child seeing them naked. Therefore, the author will offer you what he believes is the reason for Noah's anger and will use scripture to support the author's belief.

Genesis Chapter 9 tells us that Noah planted a vineyard and made wine, and he drank it until he was drunk.[46] "And he drank of the wine and was drunken; and he was uncovered within his tent. Notice that Noah is the (he) that was uncovered." Now let us examine Leviticus 18:6 None of you shall approach to any that is near of kin to him, to uncover their nakedness: I am the LORD. This means do not have sex with a near kinsman. The word uncover means have sex. Genesis 9:22 states: And Ham, the father of Canaan, saw the nakedness of his father, and told his two brethren without. The verse said that Ham saw the nakedness of his father. It did not say that Ham uncovered the nakedness of his father. Let us revisit Leviticus 18:8 which states: The nakedness of thy father's wife shalt thou not uncover: it is thy father's nakedness. That does mean that the father's nakedness is his wife. Do not have sex with your father's wife. The bible never places Ham inside the tent. Noah was inside the tent. A book called "The Legend of the Jews" states that: In his drunken condition Noah betook himself to the tent of his wife. Noah was having drunken sex with his wife and Ham saw them and watched them until they stopped and fell asleep. Then Ham went and told his brothers what he saw. Ham's brothers were not amused and respectfully covered them by walking backwards with a blanket. Noah either seen or felt Ham's presence, but he was very much into his wife at the time. Those of us who are married or have been guilty of fornication can relate to being very much into the

---

[46] Genesis 9:21 (KJV)

moment. Individuals can also relate to the man falling asleep shortly afterwards. Therefore, I am proclaiming that Noah's anger at his son Ham came from him seeing or watching his parents have drunken sex which is voyeurism a form of pornography. However, that does not explain why Noah cursed Canaan and not Ham.

First, Noah could not curse Ham because God had blessed him. Genesis 9:1 states: And God blessed Noah and his sons, and said unto them, Be fruitful, and multiply, and replenish the earth. Noah could not undo the blessing upon Ham like Isaac could not undo the blessing upon Jacob that was meant for Esau once it was given even though he was deceived. Once a blessing is given it is done. Secondly, Noah cursing Canaan was not a direct result of Ham's disrespectful observance. Noah's cursing of Canaan was revealed because of what was revealed to Noah about Canaan and he was angry with Ham. Noah was a prophet and God revealed things to Noah and prior to the incident Noah was obedient and behaved as a prophet and patriarch should. However, I speculate when Noah awoke from his wine, he revealed to Ham what was going to happen to Canaan which I believe through my research that he was supposed to keep to himself.

Please consider that prophet Noah had received revelation about what his descendants were going to do in the future. The revelations caused heaviness of heart upon Noah, and he chose to lighten his heart with drunkenness. When Noah awoke from his wine he acted out as a regular man might act. Instead of concealing revelation he revealed revelation. Notice in Genesis Chapter 9 that Noah died after revealing the curses, blessings, and enlarging of his sons and one grandson. Later in the bible Moses acted like a regular man and gave into the demands of the complaining people and because of his disobedience he was not able to enter the promise land. Henceforth, the promised land is what Canaan's curse is about.

According to the Book of Jubilees Noah's sons divided the earth unto three sections which they were to inhabit. Consider that the ark rested upon Mt. Ararat which is in modern day Turkey. The family came down from the mountains after the flood and migrated to the modern-day Middle East. Japheth and his descendants inherited the north through the Caucasus Mountains and modern-day Europe. Shem and his descendants inherited modern day Middle East and Asia and Ham, and his descendants inherited the south which is modern day Africa. Therefore, Canaan's inheritance was in the continent of Africa.

The Book of Jubilees 9: 14 states: And thus, the sons of Noah divided unto their sons in the presence of Noah their father, and he bound them all by an oath, imprecating a curse on every one that sought to seize the portion which had not fallen (to him) by his lot. Canaan and his descendants seized a land that belonged to Shem and his descendants. That is why the bible called the promise land the land of Canaan. Noah knew that Canaan was going to wickedly take land that did not belong to him. According to the Book of Jubilees Noah and his sons knew who was going to inherit each land prior to the drunken cursing episode and they all agreed upon it. Jubilees 9:15 states: And they all said, 'So be it; so be it 'for themselves and their sons forever throughout their generations till the day of judgment, on which the Lord God shall judge them with a sword and with fire for all the unclean wickedness of their errors, wherewith they have filled the earth with transgression, uncleanness, fornication, and sin. For those of us which have read and understood the bible we know that the Canaanites were considered a wicked people full of transgressions and sin to the point the Israelites the descendants of Shem were told not to intermingle or marry them. Nevertheless, this book will discuss the wickedness of the Canaanites later in this book.

According to the Book of Jubilees Noah died in the year (1659 AM). It was 29 years (1688 AM) later when Ham and his sons dispersed from the land of Shinar to occupy the portion of land they were to occupy. This was after the incident of the Tower of Babel. Jubilees 10: 29 states: And Canaan saw the land of Lebanon to the river of Egypt, that it was particularly good, and he went not into the land of his inheritance to the west (that is to) the sea, and he dwelt in the land of Lebanon, eastward and westward from the border of Jordan and from the border of the sea. Ham Canaan's father along with two of his brothers Cush (Ethiopia) and Mizraim (Egypt) told Canaan not to dwell in Shem's land but he did it anyway. Jubilees 10:32 states: Cursed art thou, and cursed shalt thou be beyond all the sons of Noah, by the curse by which we bound ourselves by an oath in the presence of the holy judge, and in the presence of Noah our father.' Therefore, Noah had revelation and prophesied that Canaan would take this land because it did not happen until 29 years after his death according to the Book of Jubilees.

Chapter 3
The Lost Tribes of Israel

The Lost Tribes of Israel is a topic without common ground from individual scholars in theorist. We do know through the bible and world history that Israel and Judah were conquered and exiled from their country around 597 B.C. by King Nebuchadnezzar of Babylon. The exact date may vary between different scholars. [47] "Israel is a scattered sheep; the lions have driven him away: first the king of Assyria hath devoured him; and last this Nebuchadnezzar king of Babylon hath broken his bones." The people of the Northern Kingdom of Israel were violently taken away from their homeland. Very few escaped but the Prophet Jeremiah was able to escape unto Egypt with select others. Daniel, Shadrach, Meshach, and Abednego did not escape captivity in Babylon. The Southern Kingdom of Judah was next to be conquered but individuals had time to escape and go into other lands. However, beyond the above mentioned there are a variation of beliefs and disputes about what happened to the tribes of Israel.

The author believes that individual Israelites dispersed into Asia, Europe, and Africa. Those who either dispersed into Europe eventually intermingled with the countries and lost their identity even though there are Europeans who claim they know who the lost tribes are. Controversially, the Israelite who were either dispersed or escaped into Asia were able to maintain their Hebrew customs and eventually migrated to Northeast Asia and crossed the Bering

---
[47] Jeremiah 50:17 (KJV)

Strait into the Americas to become the so-called Native American Indians. [48] "There is a prophecy in Amos viii. 11, 12, relative to the ten tribes of Israel while their state of banishment from the promised land, which appears exactly to accord with the account given by Esdras; and to the Indian tradition, which meets this, as will appear; and appears well to accord with the state of fact with the American natives as will be seen". Individual people in early America believed that prophecy connected Native Americans to the lost tribes of Reuben, Simeon, Dan, Naphtali, Gad, Asher, Issachar, Zebulun, Manasseh, and Ephraim, which does not have any biological, geographical, or historic evidence of still existing. However, we do know that the bible states that they will be reclaimed. [49] "Hear the word of the LORD, O ye nations, and declare it in the isles afar off, and say, He that scattered Israel will gather him, and keep him, as a shepherd doth his flock." Insomuch, people who believe bible prophecy may consider the Native American as Hebrews a possibility.

The name that continually supported the theory of Native Americans as Hebrews was from ironically from a man named Rabbi Israel. [50] "He was a Jewish spiritual leader named Rabbi Manasseh Ben Israel, who became the chief proponent of the Indians are Jews Theory and authored a famous book called Hope of Israel." The belief that Native Americans were Hebrews was widely accepted by individuals in early to mid19th century America by bible believers. A man named James Adair contributed to the Indians are Jews Theory as he traded with Indians and kept meticulous records of their Israelitish features regarding to religion and social customs. The Quaker leader William Penn was another among individuals who favored the Native Americans as being the lost tribes of Israel. However, influential people shot down this theory and swayed public opinion. In 1812 Thomas Jefferson wrote a letter to John Adams both

---

[48] Smith, Ethan. View of the Hebrews or The Ten Lost Tribes of North America. p.45
[49] Jeremiah 31:10 (KJV)
[50] Shalev, Chemi, The Mystery of the Lost Jewish Colony and Myth of the Lost Hebrew-Indian Tribes 2016.

served as President of the United States by saying that he denounced the research of James Adair's book "History of American Indians" and others who believed that Indians were Israelites as falsehood, and they only used research to support their claim. Others have called the concept absurd, fantasy, myths, or any other words to demoralize the movement and eliminate the possibility of the idea being the truth. Words by influential people can sway public opinion to line up with a leader's belief system whether their belief system is accurate or not. The topic of Native Americans as Israelites has been dormant for a long time but has not completely gone away with. Hollywood has placed minor comments in television shows and movies about the topic over the years that is overlooked. However, this book believes this topic must be reexamined because of a potential hidden agenda or propaganda to make people think and believe in a certain way.

People are taught that the bible is confusing because the Lord works in mysterious ways and therefore, we should only focus on the moral of the story. The bible can be confusing because God's ways are higher that our ways and His thoughts are higher that our thoughts but those people who choose to read, study, and ponder the scriptures God will reveal things to people as He see is fit. There are select morals to the story in the bible, but the bible is also a book of prophecy and a book of history. The bible aligns with history and individual biblical locations have been verified the archeology. There was a reason so many bible believing people believed that Native Americans were ancient Israelites. Nevertheless, let us examine why people did not and do not want to believe that Native Americans could be ancient Israelites.

It was not advantageous for the United States Government to acknowledge the Native Americans as biblical descendants of Israel because they would have to honor them and respect their property. It was more beneficial for the government to call them Indians and to paint the picture of them being savages so they could take their land without consequence and kill them if they deemed necessary without recompense. This does not mean that all people in government agreed with this, but it is possible of either a majority ruled or the most influential ruled. Secondly, we must research the contributions of Christopher Columbus to the Americas.

Christopher Columbus was made a hero for discovery America when he was really a viscous villain with crimes against humanity. Research shows that Columbus took credit for finding a land that was already inhabited by people. Columbus and his crew were documented as stealing resources, raping, and prostituting Native American women and men, enslaving, murdering people he was initially exceedingly kind to them. Furthermore, when Europeans came to the America's after 1492, they brought with them certain diseases which began to wipe out the indigenous people. Through disease and murder (genocide) more than 90 percent of the indigenous people died. Select women who survived were impregnated and had children of a lighter complexion of how they looked originally. The true history of Christopher Columbus does not tell a relevant story about the America's therefore an abbreviated and fabricated story was taught over the years to school children in America about how he set sail to America with three ships the Nina, the Pinta, and the Santa Maria. Henceforth, anyone who was taught this story in school can still recite the name of the ships decades after completing school.

Hollywood needs to be examined. Early to the late 20th century Cowboys and Indian shows and movies were extremely popular. The cowboys were always the heroes, and the Indians were usually the villains. The main exception was the television show the Lone Ranger where his side kick was an Indian named Tonto but even that show featured Indians as savages. The images from Hollywood are cemented in the minds of millions of people. This was propaganda to keep the image of Indians being savages in the minds of people and never consider the possibility of them as ancient people of God or the lost tribes of Israel. Hollywood also propagandized so called black people as savages from Africa in Tarzan movies. They were further propagandized when Americanized as being slow, lazy, criminal minded, and sneaky. Their best qualities were being good servants, good entertainers, and athletic. The propaganda of savage Indians and savage Africans or former slaves from Africa would keep people from ever conceiving that the original Hebrews may have been classified as black. The propaganda would also keep people from ever conceiving that the original Native Americans may have had darker skin before Columbus. Please do not think this is a strike against so called Caucasian or white people because it is not. There are very few that govern Hollywood and even fewer that govern world policy and views therefore so called white and black people along with Native American, Asian, Mongolian, and Latino people have been bamboozled together. Therefore, there should not be any animosity among races, however that is not the reality because the news media keeps animosity among races going.

Theoretically, all people today are the seed of Abraham in them because Abram was promised that his seed would be as sands of the sea and the stars of heaven. We also know that all people's roots trace back to Noah through his three sons Shem, Ham, and Japheth whose offspring had to intermarry with each other initially to re-populate the earth. Fortunately, what really matters if we are brothers and sister n Christ more so if we are biologically Israel.

CHAPTER 4

THE SCATTERING OF JUDAH

The scattering of Judah is a controversial issue for individuals because we have a group of people who call themselves Jewish and live in Israel today. Individual Jewish people live in America and other parts of the world. Insomuch, individual Jewish people have been successful in business, law, medicine, and entertainment (music, television, cinema) in high-ranking behind the scenes positions. People should consider that there are three ways to be considered Jewish. The first is by bloodline which is the lineage of Shem through Judah and King David. The second is by religion by either being born into or converting to the religion. The third is by location meaning that a person who lived in Judah even if they were not of the bloodline of Judah could be considered Jewish just as a person born in Israel today even if their parent's origin were different would be considered Israeli. However, for the sake of this book the author is seeking to identify the people who are lost, scattered, and do not know their lineage of being a Jew.

The Holocaust was horrific and tragic and without question a crime against humanity. The author does not favor or support the hate crimes committed against the Jewish people who suffered and lost family members or their lives during that time. No human being should have been tortured and mistreated in such a horrendous manner. With that stated I must say that what happened to the Jewish people during World War II does not align with biblical prophecy the way another group of people does in Deuteronomy Chapter 28. Henceforth, other scriptures and prophecies of the must be examined.

The bible states in multiple scripture that Judah would be scattered. [51] "Then said I, what come these to do? And he spoke, saying, these are the horns which have scattered Judah, so that no man did lift his head: but these are come to fray them, to cast out the horns of the Gentiles, which lifted their horn over the land of Judah to scatter it." The horns of the gentiles may represent the four superpowers that dominated Judah and Israel in biblical times which was Babylon, Persia, Greece, and Rome. World History coincided with biblical stories about kingdoms and conquerors. Today the main world powers are the United States, United Kingdom, France, Russia, and China each have nuclear weapons. Four other countries also have nuclear weapons Pakistan, India, North Korea, and Israel. Insomuch, the reason it is important to mention countries with nuclear weapons the modern superpowers is to see where it aligns with biblical prophecy.

The Book of Daniel talks about a beast with ten horns as well as the Book of Revelations. The author suggests that if we consider that if the ten horns represent ten nations/kingdoms that we currently have nine superpowers according to nuclear weapons (weapon of mass destruction) and that one more nation we do not know about will reveal they have nuclear capabilities. There are four kinds of weapons of mass destruction which are nuclear, radiological, chemical, and biological. Any country with a leader that is not aligned with the other superpowers (horns) may be targeted. United States President George Bush claimed that the country of Iraq lead by Saddam Hussein was said to have weapons of mass destruction and Hussein was convicted and hanged for the mistreatment of people in his country. Ironically, Iraq is the modern-day location of Babylon. [52] "And the ten horns out of this kingdom are ten kings that shall arise: and another shall rise after them; and he shall be diverse from the first,

---

[51] Zechariah 1:21 (KJV)
[52] Daniel 7:24 (KJV)

and he shall subdue three kings." In modern times the kings may be called President, Prime Minister, Chancellor, King, and other titles represent the leader of a country or kingdom. [53] "And the ten horns which thou sawest are ten kings, which have received no kingdom yet; but receive power as kings one hour with the beast." The bible tells us that the current superpowers will give their authority over to the beast or a beast system in the last/latter days. However, the bible does not list exactly who will be who in the last days.

If people could identify who the bible is referring to the scriptures would make more sense. There are a variety of groups who claim to be Judah and Israel from the bible. The groups can range from so called African Americans who claim to be Hebrew Israelites to so called white Irish people who claim that they are the lost and scattered. It became clear to the author that based upon the geographic region, period, prophecy, and other factors that the people of the bible who were of the lost tribes of Judah and Israel were people with melanin. This would make the Irish or any European claims to be Israel or Judah less likely but possible because the Israelites and Judah were dispersed to the four corners of the earth. However, upon watching a YouTube videos of so-called Black Hebrew Israelites and seeing them scream and belittle people that they did not appear to have the love of Christ in them. The so-called Black Hebrew Israelites seemed to focus on birthrights and skin color and exposing the so-called White Supremacist perspective of the bible and Christianity being all white except for Americanized slavery. Please note there are more than one sect of Hebrew Israelites in America, which most are not argumentative and not all so-called Hebrew Israelites scream and belittle people. The Good News is that all men regardless of skin color, ethnicity, or birthright can be saved. [54] "Who will have all men to be saved, and to come unto the knowledge of the truth." Therefore, birthright and having the bloodline to Israel is not exclusivity to God, but people must accept Christ to be saved.

---

[53] Revelations 17:12 (KJV)
[54] 1 Timothy 2:4 (KJV)

It should be noted that Jesus said who He thought he was coming for when speaking to a Canaanite woman before seeing her faith. God has a covenant with Judah and Israel that He will honor. Judah and Israel are referred to as the lost sheep. Jesus knew that He was sent to reclaim the lost sheep of Israel before He acknowledged that he would be the gateway to reclaim all mankind. [55] "But he answered and said, I am not sent but unto the lost sheep of the house of Israel." When a person is lost, they are at a place that is foreign to their origins and may not know who they are or where they are. When Jesus recognized the faith of a person not in covenant with Him salvation became available to all that had faith in Him. The author believes that Jesus was disappointed by the lack of faith in Israel/Judah and how non covenant people showed more faith than His so-called people. [56] "When Jesus heard it, he marveled, and said to them that followed, Verily I say unto you, I have not found so great faith, no, not in Israel." The faith of individual Gentiles made them worthy of salvation with a bloodline covenant person who believes and over a bloodline covenant person who did not believe. [57] "There is neither Jew nor Greek, there is neither bond nor free, there is neither male nor female: for ye are all one in Christ Jesus." Nevertheless, in the last days Judah that was scattered will have lost their identity or had their identity unjustly taken from them and Christ will reclaim them and restore them as promised in the scriptures.

One must ask the question where are the Jews in modern times that Christ is supposed to restore? We have people today that say that they are the Jews of the bible. However, they have reclaimed habitation in Jerusalem, Israel, and reside in other parts of the world knowing who they are and choosing where they reside. Therefore, these people are neither lost nor scattered. The author's research found that modern Jewish people in Israel and Ashkenazi are Jews through the mother's genealogy, but the author will say that they are not the people of the father's genealogy that the Book of Isaiah and Jeremiah

---

[55] Matthew 15:24 (KJV)
[56] Matthew 8:10 (KJV)
[57] Galatians 3:28 (KJV)

were prophesying about. Select people in Israel could be the people that the Book of Revelation was prophesying about. Henceforth, let us examine the possibilities of the modern-day people from Judah.

The author believes that the modern-day Jews should be treated with profound respect in the same manner that David respected King Saul. Saul initially admired David but he grew to resent David and wanted to kill him according to the bible. Despite Saul's efforts to destroy David he never disrespected Saul's position as king. David knew that he was anointed to be the next king, but he was willing to wait until God placed him in the position as king. David knew that if he would have killed Saul when he had the opportunity to that may have lost the blessings of God the way Saul lost his anointing because of disobedience. 1 Samuel 26: 11 stated that David was forbidden to stretch forth his hand against the Lord's anointed. Furthermore, David was also close to Saul's son Johnathan, and they loved each other as brothers. David looked out for any remaining descendants of Saul and Johnathan after their deaths not to destroy them as other kings would but to bring them to his house and give them an inheritance. Therefore, if so-called African Americans are the actual descendants of Judah, it would be wise to have the heart and attitude of the future King David and let the Lord do His will as He sees fit. [58] "Dearly beloved, avenge not yourselves, but give place unto wrath: for it is written, Vengeance is mine; I will repay, saith the Lord." Henceforth, David showed great patience, respect, and love during adversity and jealous pursuit of King Saul.

It should be noted that the bible clearly states in Revelations 2:9 and Revelations 3:9 that a people are posing as Jews but are not. Therefore, there has been identity theft among the people on earth. However, the author does not believe that all parties who are titled Jews are beneficiaries of the conspiracy. The bible is referring did not say it was all people who claim to be Jewish. The author speculates (opinion) it is less than 1% of approximately fifteen million Jews. The bible called out the pretending Jews who are not bloodline connected

---

[58] Romans 12:19 (KJV)

to the mother or fathers' genealogy who are rich, elite, and controlling people who despise Jesus. [59] "I know thy works, and tribulation, and poverty, (but thou art rich) and I know the blasphemy of them which say they are Jews, and are not, but are the synagogue of Satan." To say that someone is of the synagogue of Satan is powerful statement against people who obviously oppose God. [60] "Behold, I will make them of the synagogue of Satan, which say they are Jews, and are not, but do lie; behold, I will make them to come and worship before thy feet, and to know that I have loved thee." Jesus is referring to a future event that those of the synagogue of Satan will not only be exposed for their lies but will be humbled before the world. The author is making it clear that based upon his research that the bible is not talking about all people who have the ethnicity title of Jew belonging to the synagogue of Satan nevertheless many individuals have prospered from wearing the title of being a Jew. Insomuch, the father bloodline Jews of the bible are lost and scattered and do not know who they are with a select individuals are starting to wake up and discover who they are or may be in the newly found so-called information age.

The author is going to use a sports/football comparison to explain the Jews of the bible and the Jews in the world today. There is a football team in Ohio called the Cleveland Browns. The Cleveland Browns were originally established in 1944 but did not begin playing games until 1946 after World War II ended. The Browns had a rich history including Hall of Fame Players and won four championships between 1950 and 1964. A man named Art Modell bought the Cleveland Browns in 1961 and in the 1990s he wanted the mother city of Cleveland to build him a new stadium which they refused to do for years. He got tired of the city of Cleveland not giving in to his request and he moved the team to Baltimore in 1996 and gave them a new name and called them the Baltimore Ravens. The mother city of Cleveland was distraught and was without a football

---

[59] Revelations 2:9 (KJV)
[60] Revelations 3:9 (KJV)

team for three years. In 1999 the National Football League (NFL) created an expansion team and called them the Cleveland Browns. The city regained a football team, but the true father history of the team technically follows the team called the Baltimore Ravens. However, the new expansion team took the history of the original franchise and claimed it as its own. The people we recognize today as the Ashkenazi Jews are like the expansion team that is now called the Cleveland Browns. The biblical Jews are like the Baltimore Ravens who has the true father history but is not recognized as the original. People who are born after 1996 when Art Modell moved the Browns to Baltimore would not have a memory of the original Browns. People who do not research the historical records of the NFL will never know the difference. Ironically, people who do not read and study the bible for themselves will not come to the truth of God's word until they/ if they ever seek biblical knowledge.

The author's research shows that the descendants of the scattered Judah are so-called black people in America. Not all so-called black people are from Judah but could be from Semitic from the Tribe of Israel, Hebrew from Abraham, or a Hamite from Africa. Unfortunately, bloodline birthright does not equate salvation but can increase pride. Pride and sin were the reason that Judah and Israel lost the protection of the Most High God. [61] "Thus, saith the LORD, After this manner will I mar the pride of Judah, and the immense pride of Jerusalem." Sin is the reason that Judah and Israel stopped receiving the knowledge of God to protect them from themselves. [62] "My people are destroyed for lack of knowledge: because thou hast rejected knowledge, I will also reject thee, that thou shalt be no priest to me: seeing thou hast forgotten the law of thy God, I will also forget thy children." God acknowledges that he had a people, but the people did not live their part of the covenant that Abraham made with God. Therefore, God removed His covering of protection from over the people of Judah and Israel to teach and remind them

---

[61] Jerimiah 13:9 (KJV)
[62] Hosea 4:6 (KJV)

of who He is to them. Therefore, the original people of Judah and Israel are a people who are suffering or of lowly socio-economic status in general today.

The so-called scattered Judah can be found in every nation. However, except for select countries in the continent of Africa so-called black people are considered socially less than Caucasian people or lighter skinned people in the same nation. In the United States there are individual prominent so-called black people through various respectable fields/careers but especially entertainment and athletics. The so-called black people who are socially and career wise successful are viewed as an exception to the rule. So called black people would never be considered the chosen and cursed people of the bible because of disobedience and rejection of God's will for them. The American society as a majority would reject the possibility of Judah being non-white. The author does not believe that most people are hateful or racist it is because there have been images engraved upon our minds such as the image of Christ as painted by Leonardo Da Vinci.

There are a variety of books that have been written that describe how people with melanin came to the Americas. The books that most solidified the author's perspective are "From Babylon to Timbuktu" by Rudolph Windsor, "Into Egypt Again with Ships" by Elisha Israel, "They Came Before Columbus" by Ivan Van Sertima, "Hidden in Plain Sight" by Huldah Dauid, and "Hebrews to Negroes" by Ronald Dalton Jr. Each of the five previously listed books has excerpts in them that discusses the Trans-Atlantic traveling from the African continent to the Americas. The late Pastor Stephen Darby of Destined Ministries in Louisville, Ky created a video called Negroland which had a profound impact on the author of this book. In the video he made select interesting points one of the first impactful points was about the word negro in the well-respected Zondervan's Compact Bible Dictionary. [63] "{"Ham: The youngest son of Noah, born probably about 96 years before the Flood; and one

---

[63] Zondervan Bible Dictionary

of eight persons to live through the Flood. He became the progenitor of the dark races; **not the Negroes**, but the Egyptians, Ethiopians, Libyans and Canaanites." – Zondervan Bible Dictionary". Prior to the author watching the video and researching for himself he never would have considered the Negro being anything but an African or a descendant of Ham. So called blacks and whites had the same perspective that negroes were blacks that came from Africa. In the beginning of the popular television mini- series called "Roots" by Alex Haley there were scenes which showed African males help European/American slave catchers capture other African males and females to become slaves. Africans were betraying their own people. Pastor Darby and four of the authors of the previously mentioned books made the point that the Africans knew that the negroes were not descendants of Ham and were not selling or helping to catch their own people. Henceforth, if the negroes are not from Noah's son Ham, then from whom are they?

The bible refers in Genesis Chapter 10 that Japheth was the father of the gentiles. [64] "By these were the isles of the Gentiles divided in their lands; everyone after his tongue, after their families, in their nations." According to the map the continent of Europe in the Mediterranean Sea is full of small islands especially around Greece, Turkey, and Italy. The bible did not call the people of Shem or Ham gentiles. That would leave Noah's son Shem as the father of the negroes. This would also explain why in the Book of Genesis that Abraham, Isaac, Jacob, and their offspring where able to blend with the crowd in Egypt which are descendants of Ham because they both would be considered black people based upon their skin color. The difference between the sons of Ham and sons of Shem is that Ham's sons were paganistic and Shem's sons believed and were in covenant with The Most High God. However, let us focus specifically upon Judah and how they became lost and scattered.

The tribe of Judah springs from one of Jacob/Israel's sons. Judah was the third born son of Jacob and Leah who was foretold by Jacob/

---

[64] Genesis 10:5 (KJV)

Israel to he would be the one his brothers would praise. [65] "Judah, thou art he whom thy brethren shall praise: thy hand shall be in the neck of thine enemies; thy father's children shall bow down before thee." Jacob/Israel prophesied of Judah's strength on his death bed. [66] "Judah is a lion's whelp: from the prey, my son, thou art gone up: he stooped down, he couched as a lion, and as an old lion; who shall rouse him up? Finally, Jacob/Israel prophesied that Judah's lineage would be special."[67] "The sceptre shall not depart from Judah, nor a lawgiver from between his feet, until Shiloh come; and unto him shall the gathering of the people be." Individual scholars believe that until Shiloh comes is referring until the Messiah Jesus Christ returns. Biblical history shows that Jesus' lineage comes through Judah as did King David as the Christ is sometimes referred to as the son of David or the son of man. Also, the Book of Genesis prophesied that Judah's people would be scattered because they would need to be gathered. Henceforth, let us examine why Judah was scattered.

The children of Judah began fleeing Jerusalem and Israel since the time of Nebuchadnezzar since he invaded the Northern Kingdom of Israel and took tribes to Babylon around 597 B.C. However, the last great migration came around 70 A.D. when the Romans invaded and destroyed Jerusalem. [68] "In 70 A.D. General Vespasian and his son, Titus put an end to the Jewish state with a great slaughter". Roman General Pompay had took control over Jerusalem 5 years earlier before the great slaughter and over a period individual Black Jews were sold into slavery. [69] "During the period from Pompay to Julius, it has been estimated that over one million Jews fled to Africa, fleeing from Roman persecution and slavery." [70] "The Jews dispersed to various areas in Africa. Other Jews fled to areas where Romans did not have authority, this was the region of the south, the

---

[65] Genesis 49:8 (KJV)
[66] Genesis 49:9 (KJV)
[67] Genesis 49:10 (KJV)
[68] From Babylon to Timbuktu, Windsor, Rudolph. pg. 84
[69] From Babylon to Timbuktu, Windsor, R. pg. 84
[70] From Babylon to Timbuktu, Windsor, R. pg. 86

Sahara Desert, and the Sudan."[71] "Before Solomon's Temple was destroyed in 70 A.D. the remaining scattered Israelites still knew their heritage despite a history of captivity to the Egyptians, Assyrians, Babylonians, Persians, Greeks, and Romans." According to research gathered by Elisha J. Israel from Robert Dolezal the persecution of the Jews was merciless.[72] "During this siege, the Romans showed no mercy executing as up to five hundred Jews a day." Henceforth, as time continued and Jews migrated, they began to establish their culture in Africa.

According to the research of Dr. Rudolph Windsor and Ronald Dalton Jr. they gave great details about different civilizations that were created in Africa by the Jews who fled Roman oppression.[73] "In select Medieval African Maps (500 A.D. to 1500 A.D) there can be seen the word "Negroland" above "Guinea" in an area known as West Africa." The term Negroland no longer exist on African maps.[74] "In the 1729 map titled "Negroland and Guinea" anyone can see that these two regions comprised West Africa where African slaves (aka Hebrew Israelites) were taken to be scattered into nations of the West. In the 1700s Africa was divided between England, Denmark, and Holland (Dutch)." Prior to watching the Stephen Darby video on Negroland the author never heard of the location. Upon the author's research he found that you can Google 1729 or 1747 map of Negroland, and it will come up in the search engine. Insomuch, one must question why most people are unaware of the Negroland and why did it disappear.

The author believes that here was a conscience effort to conceal Negroland because someone did not want so-called African American or Black people to find out that they had a heritage beyond the narrative of savages being taken from a jungle to become slaves in America. Today the term negro is rarely used in general. One could assume the word negro is too close to the derogatory term used to

---

[71] Hebrews to Negroes, Dalton Jr., Ronald pg. 266
[72] Into Egypt Again With Ships, Israel, Elisha J. pg. 26
[73] Hebrews to Negroes, Dalton Jr., R. pg. 70
[74] Hebrews to Negroes, Dalton Jr., R. pg. 72

negatively refer to a person of color. However, slavery during the 16, 17, and 1800s must be evaluated.

Slavery in the Americas was not aligned with servitude in the bible. Slaves in the bible had rights, they were able to have a family, read, educate their children, and they could become free after years of service. American slaves during the 16, 17, and 1800s were not allowed to read, had their original names stripped and given new European names, and depending on the kindness or cruelty of the masters had their families divided while being treated like chattel property. The author is not displaying animosity but simply stating the research of slavery in America. The slaves that came to America and after gaining freedom resemble the curses of Deuteronomy 28 like no other group of people on the planet. The author wants to emphasize that he believes that America is a great country because it allows religious freedoms and re-emphasize the fact that a pure race does not exist on planet earth because despite our physical appearance all people came off Noah's ark and have blended bloodlines consisting of each of Noah's three sons. However, the world places heavy emphasis on physical appearance which includes skin color, race, ethnicity, and genetics.

The author's research about the lost and scattered tribe of Judah made select interesting discoveries. The most convincing evidence did not come from so-called black people but so called white and caramel colored people. [75] "Former Egyptian President Gamel Abdel Nassar (1956-1970) was rumored to have stated: "You (Jews) will never be able to live here in peace, because you left here black and came back white." – Gamal Abdel Nasser." The video of the broadcast is no longer available which means it cannot be proven as a true statement. The actual video of Egyptian President is unavailable at my last search and there are sources that dispute that he ever made the claim. American Journalist Helen Thomas made a comment about Jews

---

[75] Meme. https://me.me/i/2nd-president-of-egypt-gamal-abdel-nasser-you-jews-will-15406580

that brought her under fire. [76] "Helen Thomas a former dean of the White House press corps, after announcing that she is "retiring" as a Hearst columnist following controversial comments in which she said Israeli Jews should return "home" to Poland and Germany and give the land back to the Palestinians." Due to her comment about the Israeli's, she was pressured into giving a rebuttal. [77] "I deeply regret my comments I made last week regarding the Israelis and the Palestinians." They do not reflect my heart-felt belief that peace will come to the Middle East only when all parties recognize the need for mutual respect and tolerance. May that day come soon." Thomas who was considered Caucasian and born in America to parents of Lebanese descent made comments in 2010 that shows that people in the world are aware that Jews in modern day Israel are not the same Jews from biblical Israel. However, the author wants to take notice to the reactions to anyone who says anything against the people who are called Jewish today.

There are laws in the United States regarding anti-Semitism. The definition of Anti-Semitism on American soil is quite extensive. [78] "The following is a list from U.S. Department of State defining Anti- Semitism:

- Calling for, aiding, or justifying the killing or harming of Jews in the name of a radical ideology or an extremist view of religion.
- Making mendacious, dehumanizing, demonizing, or stereotypical allegations about Jews as such or the power of Jews as collective — such as, especially but not exclusively, the myth about a world Jewish conspiracy or of Jews controlling the media, economy, government, or other societal institutions.

---

[76] James, Frank. https://www.npr.org/sections/thetwo-way/2010/06/helen_thomas_retires_after_ant.html

[77] James, F. https://www.npr.org/sections/thetwo-way/2010/06/helen_thomas_retires_after_ant.html

[78] U.S. Department of State. https://www.state.gov/defining-anti-semitism/

- Accusing Jews as a people of being responsible for real or imagined wrongdoing committed by a single Jewish person or group, or even for acts committed by non-Jews.
- Denying the fact, scope, mechanisms (e.g., gas chambers) or intentionality of the genocide of the Jewish people at the hands of National Socialist Germany and its supporters and accomplices during World War II (the Holocaust)
- Accusing the Jews as a people, or Israel as a state, of inventing or exaggerating the Holocaust.
- Accusing Jewish citizens of being more loyal to Israel, or to the alleged priorities of Jews worldwide, than to the interests of their own nations.
- Denying the Jewish people their right to self-determination, e.g., by claiming that the existence of a State of Israel is a racist endeavor.
- Applying double standards by requiring of it a behavior not expected or demanded of any other democratic nation.
- Using the symbols and images associated with classic antisemitism (e.g., claims of Jews killing Jesus or blood libel) to characterize Israel or Israelis.
- Drawing comparisons of contemporary Israeli policy to that of the Nazis.
- Holding Jews collectively responsible for actions of the state of Israel."

Upon the author reviewing the definition and actions of anti-Semitism a person should be afraid to say or do anything against the people who call themselves Jewish. No other so-called race or nationality has a detailed description of hate crimes against them. People in America say the worst things about the different Presidents of the United States and will not suffer the label or prosecution that one could face speaking against the modern Jewish people. All races and nationalities have various tasteless jokes and negative stereotypes that can be expressed without being criminally prosecuted. Dumb blonde and stupid jock jokes are also commonplace but again not consequence of criminal prosecution. The author has no desire to speak negatively about the Jewish people but is simply observing how people must back track statements if they speak anything perceived negative about the Jewish people or face backlash or persecution for their comments. Insomuch, the author is re-affirming his position that the curses of Deuteronomy 28 correlate with people in America that are currently called African American and nobody else on the planet timeline and history aligns as perfect.

Elisha J. Israel authored a book titled "Into Egypt Again With Ships" which is directly correlated to Deuteronomy 28: 68. [79] "And the Lord shall bring thee into Egypt again with ships, whereof I said unto thee, Thou shalt see it no more again: and there ye shall sell yourselves unto your enemies for bondmen and bondwomen, and there *shall be* no buyer." [80] "Individual people, including select American Blacks, regard the notion of Jesus and the Israelites as black as nothing more than a feeble attempt to instill pride in the Black race." The author admits that he had similar thoughts and doubted the possibility of Jesus, Israelites, and Jews as possibly being black as nonsense. The Trans-Atlantic Trade is how individual people equate how Africans came to America. [81] "There is much proof, and still much more to be revealed by scholars, that there existed prior to the slave trade and after its Jewish tribes, colonies, and kingdoms in West Africa." [82] "It is the conclusion of individual scholars that when the Jewish kingdom of Ghana fell, individual Hebrew tribes established settlements among the African tribes throughout central and western Africa.' It is believed that Africans could distinguish the Jewish or Hebrew tribes from Hamite African tribes. In other words, they could distinguish between the sons of Ham and the sons of Shem. The sons of Shem eventually lost their identity and knowing who they were. [83] "Like the black Jews in America, individual Jews of Guinea do not

---

[79] Deuteronomy 28:68 (KJV)
[80] Into Egypt Again With Ships, Israel, E. pg. 10
[81] From Babylon to Timbuktu, Windsor, R. pg. 121
[82] From Babylon to Timbuktu, Windsor, R. pg. 121
[83] From Babylon to Timbuktu, Windsor, R. pg. 123

remember their original nationality." [84] "This deplorable ignorance is attributed to various causes: 91) The fall of the Hebrew Kingdom, (2) the lack of communication with Jewish educational centers (3) intense persecution, and deliberate blotting out of the mind of their true nationality." However, as the author researched and investigated there appeared to be an attempt to suppress certain information about history and genealogy.

The bible prophesied about the fall of the people of Judah in the Book of Isaiah. [85] "And he shall set up an ensign for the nations, and shall assemble the outcasts of Israel, and gather the dispersed of Judah from the four corners of the earth." People who are considered an outcast or dispersed are not people in a power position in the world. Today in the United States we have people of various nationalities, ethnicities, and race who have wealth and fame. Athletes and entertainers' faces may become well known however it is the owners that have the real power who usually remain unseen and less famous. Nevertheless, the real battle is not so much against people, but a system designed for certain people to excel and most people to struggle. [86] "For we wrestle not against flesh and blood, but against principalities, against powers, against the rulers of the darkness of this world, against spiritual wickedness in high places." The power system of this world will hate people in covenant with God even those who do not know their ancestors were once covenanted with God. The media contributes to the mindset of people. [87] "Wherein in time past ye walked according to the course of this world, according to the prince of the power of the air, the spirit that now worketh in the children of disobedience." The power of the air is radio, television, movies, music, and the internet and the prince of the air is Satan. The early to mid-20th century media only portrayed good so-called blacks and Indians as sidekicks or submissive roles, otherwise they

---

[84] From Babylon to Timbuktu, Windsor, R. pg. 123
[85] Isaiah 11:12 (KJV)
[86] Ephesians 6:12 (KJV)
[87] Ephesians 2:2 (KJV)

were betrayed as violent savages or in the case of blacks' ignorant buffoons. Mostly, that has changed but damage and imagery was set.

Hollywood and other media outlets do an excellent job setting public opinion. Anything that contradicts the preset images will face great resistance. Through research the author believes that the scattered tribes of Judah are black. Former Egyptian President Gamel Abdel Nassar made the statement Israel left black and came back white. He was not the only person overseas who thought that but because of his position he thought his statement could have a larger impact. The media was not kind to him according to other videos that the author viewed about him. Helen Thomas was a respected White House journalist she also referred to the people currently in Israel not being the biblical Israel. The media was not kind to her, and she was forced to make a statement to soften the impact of her statement. She was not the only Caucasian to make a statement, but she had profound influence because she represented the media. Ironically, in both cases nobody accused either person of lying. The claims were buried by the media so they would not receive attention to create a discussion. They way Nassar and Thomas were treated created fear for anyone else to make any similar claims about who is and who is not Jewish. Insomuch, the author has concerns about his claims about who Judah is and if there will be any repercussions.

Part Two
Biblical Genealogy

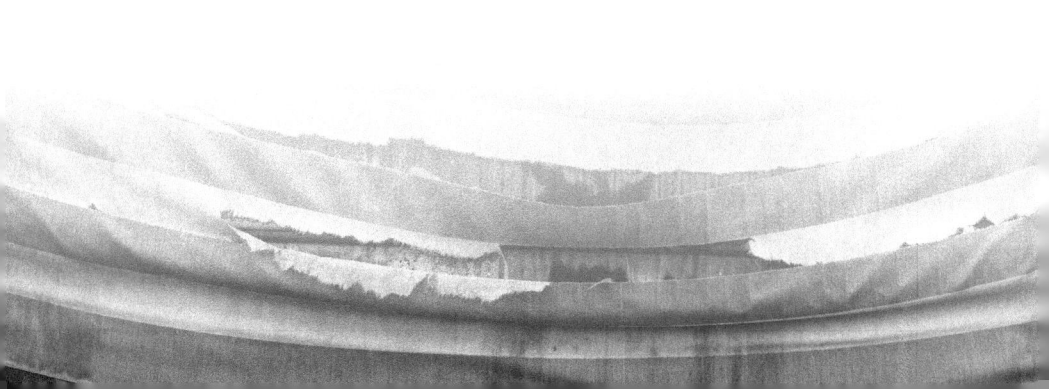

Chapter 5
Connections to the Patriarchs

The Book of Genesis Chapter 1 provides us with the information about God creating our world. The author believes the biblical accounts of the creation of the world and rejects the "The Big Bang Theory" and "The Theory of Evolution." However, that is not to say that the author rejects science or the evolution of people. Science, Geography, Geology, Architecture, and Genetics has proven the truthfulness of the bible while science simply explains how God created the things in this world. Chapter 5 will focus on the lineage connections of the Patriarchs of the bible. Insomuch, one must focus on the beginning and the creation of man.

Genesis Chapter 1 tells us of the creation of man. [88] "And God said, let us make man in our image, after our likeness: and let them have dominion over the fish of the sea, and over the fowl of the air, and over the cattle, and over all the earth, and over every creeping thing that creepeth upon the earth." God created the spirit of man and gave him a purpose before creating his physical body. The author believes that the "us" in creation is the Father, The Son, and The Holy Ghost. [89] "So, God created man in his own image, in the image of God created he him; male and female created he them." If God created males and females prior to giving them physical bodies that must mean that the spirit of a man is far more important, then

---

[88] Genesis 1:26 (KJV)
[89] Genesis 1:27 (KJV)

the physical attributes of a man. God gave the commandment to be fruitful and to multiply before coming to earth along with having the ability to have dominion over the earth. Henceforth, let us examine the creation of the human body.

The human body comes from the earth. Purpose for man is why God placed a man on earth. [90] "And every plant of the field before it was in the earth, and every herb of the field before it grew: for the LORD God had not caused it to rain upon the earth, and there was not a man to till the ground." God created everything that man would need prior to placing him on earth. [91] "But there went up a mist from the earth and watered the whole face of the ground." Notice that God watered the earth prior to forming him and consider that humans are around 70% water. Ironically, the earth is also about 70% water and was present before the land was formed. [92] "And the LORD God formed man of the dust of the ground and breathed into his nostrils the breath of life; and man became a living soul." The first man Adam was the patriarch of all men created by God from the earth. The woman created by God was the first surgery. [93] "And the LORD God caused a deep sleep to fall upon Adam, and he slept: and he took one of his ribs and closed the flesh instead thereof." The woman that we call Eve was created with the purpose of being a helpmeet for man. The bible tells us of the creation of the human body and original parents of us all. Before man was created on earth as stated in Genesis 1:26 man was commanded to be fruitful and multiple in other words have sex with your spouse and bear children. Henceforth, the patriarchal connection begins with Adam.

Genesis Chapter 5 gives the genealogy of ten generations from Adam to Noah. The author finds it important to address that all people on earth today come from this lineage regardless of a person's race or ethnicity. God did not create a separate set of people to form different races and ethnicities. Sunday Schools, bible studies, and individuals

---

[90] Genesis 2: 5 (KJV)
[91] Genesis 2: 6 (KJV)
[92] Genesis 2:7 (KJV)
[93] Genesis 2:21 (KJV)

either overlook or skip over Genesis 5:4.[94] "And the days of Adam after he had begotten Seth were eight hundred years: and he begat sons and daughters." Adam and Eve had other children besides Cain, Abel, and Seth. The issue that the author believes was intentionally overlooked was the fact that to be fruitful and multiple brothers and sisters had to become husbands and wives, which we know today as incest. Incest is frowned upon in today's culture, insomuch in today the world is diverse enough and populated enough that we should not engage with near kin. The Book of Leviticus Chapter 18 gives examples of inappropriate sexual relationships which forbids brother and sister sexual relationships. However, at the beginning of the world that was the only way to populate the earth because there was only a minimum amount of people. The same was true with Noah and his three sons and their wives. In Noah's days after the flood his grandchildren may have set the standard for cousin-to-cousin marriages but there may have been sibling marriages, uncle and niece marriages and other combinations that would be frowned upon today. Insomuch, after the flood repopulation of the earth people were able to distance their kinsmen connections.

The Patriarch Abram/Abraham was born before the law of Moses denounced sibling marriages, and he married Saria/Sarah who was his half-sister. Abraham was guilty of lying in the bible, but he was really being deceiving and not telling the whole truth to Pharoah out of fear of losing his life. Sarai was beautiful physically and Abram feared that the Egyptians would kill him to take his wife from him. [95] "Say, I pray thee, thou art my sister: that it may be well with me for thy sake; and my soul shall live because of thee." Pharoah house was plagued because of the deception which caused Pharoah to become upset and address Abram. [96] "Why saidst thou, she is my sister? so I might have taken her to me to wife: now therefore behold thy wife, take her, and go thy way." Nevertheless, later in the bible the Lord blessed Abram and changed his name to Abraham and his wife's

---

[94] Genesis 5:4 (KJV)
[95] Genesis 12:13 (KJV)
[96] Genesis 12:19 (KJV)

name from Saria to Sarah as Abraham was promised to be the father of many nations before he had any children.

Abraham became the patriarch with a promise from the Lord. [97] "Neither shall thy name any more be called Abram, but thy name shall be Abraham; for a father of nations have I made thee." [98] "And I will make thee exceed fruitful, and I will make nations of thee, and kings shall come out of thee." The relationship between Abraham and the Lord led to a commitment between the Lord and the seed of Abraham because of the faithfulness of Abraham. [99] "And I will establish my covenant between me and thee and thy seed after thee in their generations for an everlasting covenant, to be a God unto thee, and to thy seed after thee." However, even though the Lord promised rich blessings to Abraham's seed he also warned him about the future struggles and tough times.

The Lord promised Abraham a certain land to inherit that they had yet to possess. [100] "And I will give unto thee, and to thy seed after thee, the land wherein thou art a stranger, all the land of Canaan, for an everlasting possession; and I will be their God." The Lord also warned Abraham that his seed would be enslaved. [101] "And he said unto Abram, know of a surety that thy seed shall be a stranger in a land that is not theirs, and shall serve them; and they shall afflict them four hundred years." Abram's relationship with the Lord God of Hosts was special and the information provided to Abram happened in the Book of Exodus. [102] "Now the sojourning of the children of Israel, who dwelt in Egypt, was four hundred and thirty years."

In the bible Abraham was given a promise and prophecy that his seed was as the stars of the sky and the sand of the sea. [103] "That in blessing I will bless thee, and in multiplying I will multiply thy seed

---

[97] Genesis 17:5 (KJV)
[98] Genesis 17:6 (KJV)
[99] Genesis 17:7 (KJV)
[100] Genesis 17:8 (KJV)
[101] Genesis 15:13 (KJV)
[102] Exodus 12:40 (KJV)
[103] Genesis 22:17 (KJV)

as the stars of the heaven, and as the sand which is upon the seashore; and thy seed shall possess the gate of his enemies." Insomuch, we are not able to count the number of Abraham's seed. It is very possible that somewhere in each person's genealogy can be traced back to Abraham. Consider that every person who has ever lived has had two biological parents, four biological grandparents, eight biological great grandparents, sixteen biologicals great- great- grandparents, and so forth which is five generations. Ten generations such as from Adam to Noah consisted of 512 parents. Each person's 21st generation consists of over one million different parents 1,048,560 different people to be exact assuming that fathers were not impregnating their daughters which would skew the numbers. If we guestimate an average age for each generation of twenty-five that would mean that ten generations would be approximately 250 years. Depending on the family line the average generation line would vary because families have a history of teenage parenting while other families may have children in their thirties and individual men up to their 50s, 60s, and older. Therefore, twenty-one generations of one million plus different parents for each person would go back and average of 530 years. Jesus Christ walked this earth over two thousand years ago and Abraham was two thousand years before Christ. Therefore, it is difficult to estimate how different parental multiple greats it would take to trace back to Abraham.

Human behavior has not changed since biblical days. [104] "The thing that hath been, it is that which shall be and that which is done is that which shall be done: and there is no new thing under the sun." Today we see multiple children from interracial marriages, different ethnicities, different religions, and other differences and insomuch what we see today was happening back in Abraham's era. In Abraham's era he did not want his offspring to intermarry with the Canaanites. Later the Ammonites and Moabites would join that list for the Hebrews not to intermarry however despite the instructions from the Patriarchs Hebrews still intermarried with the forbidden

---

[104] Ecclesiastes 1:19 (KJV)

people. Esau was the first notable person to disobey the request not to intermarry with the Canaanites however even Judah whose lineage leads to the savior also dishonored the request. Matthew Chapter 1 begins with the genealogy of Jesus through his stepfather Joseph. The Book of Luke Chapter 3 gives what is believed to be the genealogy of Jesus through His biological mother Mary. In each case you can find women who were from forbidden family lines as part of the saviors genetic DNA. Therefore, if Jesus Christ did not have a pure bloodline, we may assume that nobody on earth has a so-called pure bloodline.

The origin of racial identity can be easily hidden over time as well. For instance, if two parents, where one is so-called black and one is so-called white, have a child the child will choose a spouse and have children when of age. If a mixed child marries a so-called white person and their children continue to marry so-called white people, the identity of the black parent will be lost as far as physical appearance. The same is true the other way around if a mixed child chooses a spouse who is a so-called black person, and their children continue to marry so-called black people their white identity will be lost in physical appearance over time. Individual people spend too much time judging a person's physical appearance and race and disregard the fact that we all come from the ark of Noah and therefore all come from Adam who came from God. God is concerned about our connection and relationship to Him and not how we look or identify ourselves. However, God does honor His covenants with mankind, and He does not forget them even when His covenant people are suffering. God made a covenant with Abraham, Isaac, and Jacob. [105] "And God heard their groaning, and God remembered his covenant with Abraham, with Isaac, and with Jacob." When God's covenant people suffer is usually when the people forget or ignore their covenant with God and are living like the people around them. When the people dishonor their covenant with God, they lose their protection and often fall into slavery or servitude. However, God

---

[105] Exodus 2:24 (KJV)

is good to restore his protection to future generations that cry out unto Him.

God loves all His children covenant or not as we are all His children in this world. God knew that we would need a savior because of our flesh which is worldly. [106] "For God so loved the world, that he gave his only begotten Son, that whosoever believeth in him should not perish, but have everlasting life." Therefore, it is by faith and belief in the son Jesus Christ that we are grafted into salvation and are part of the Patriarchal lineage of Abraham, Isaac, and Jacob. However, those who choose not to believe in Jesus Christ will not be grafted in even those who were of the biological lineage are a broken branch if they do not believe. [107] "And they also, if they abide not still in unbelief, shall be grafted in for God is able to graft them in again." Therefore, our belief and our faith in the Word is more important than lineage.

---

[106] John 3:16 (KJV)
[107] Romans 11:23 (KJV)

CHAPTER 6
THE TWO NATIONS OF JACOB AND ESAU

The reason the two nations of Jacob and Esau is separated is because of the distinction the bible makes between the two in the last days. In both the New and Old Testaments stated that God loves Jacob but hated Esau in the Book of Romans and the Book of Malachi. [108] "As it is written, Jacob have I loved, but Esau have I hated." In the Book of Malachi, it used two verses to make the same claim about the Lord's perspective. One must ask why did God love Jacob but hated Esau? When the bible is describing Jacob and Esau as far as love and hate it is referring to their descendants and not the two brothers. In the bible Esau did desire to kill Jacob but after years of not seeing each other when they met the embraced each other. [109] "I have loved you, saith the LORD. Yet ye say, wherein hast thou loved us? Was not Esau Jacob's brother? saith the LORD: yet I loved Jacob." The author believes that the God could be referring to spiritual Jacob and Esau meaning that Jacob values and loves the ways of God and Esau despises God and loves the ways of the world which are directed by Satan and mammon (money). [110] "And I hated Esau and laid his mountains and his heritage waste for the dragons of the wilderness." Individual people believe that God is love which contradicts the

---

[108] Romans 9:13 (KJV)
[109] Malachi 1:2 (KJV)
[110] Malachi 1:3 (KJV)

belief that God can hate. Nevertheless, the bible clearly states in Malachi and Romans that God hated Esau.

The Book of Genesis tells us that two nations were in Isaac's wife Rebekah which were Jacob and Esau. The bible tells us that the twins were fighting inside of the womb, and they battled to see who would come out first. Esau was born first, and he was a hairy man of the field. He valued things of the world. Jacob was a smooth man and what individual people using slang would call today a "momma's boy." Jacob was a quick thinker and somewhat of a trickster meaning that he was an opportunist who took advantage of situations to get what he wanted. One such situation the bible spoke of was Esau returning from the field hungry. The idea that Jacob was a quick thinker comes from the story in the bible in Genesis chapter 25 where Jacob took advantage of Esau's hunger and asked Esau to sell his birthright for his red pottage. Esau's reply was that his birthright did not mean anything if he died from hunger. The idea that Jacob was a trickster came from the bible story in Genesis where he allowed his mother to convince him to trick his father Isaac unto believing he was Esau. He tricked his father by putting on Esau's clothes, putting animal hair on his arms to appear hairy to his blind father, and presenting a meal prepared and seasoned by his mother Rebekah to appear as venison that Esau was asked to go hunt. Upon the deception of Jacob his father gave him the blessing that Isaac intended and believed that he was giving Esau. Not only was Jacob a trickster but Rebekah was too as well as her brother Laban who later in the Book of Genesis deceived and tricked Jacob until his spiritual maturity grew. Insomuch, when Esau returned with the last wish meal for his father and found out that his blessing was given to Jacob, he was hurt which turned to great anger towards Jacob.

Esau intended to wait for his father Isaac to die so he could kill Jacob. Rebekah sent Jacob away to her brother Laban to spare his life from Esau's intentions to kill him. Jacob was fearful of his brother Esau. Jacob prayed and sought God to deliver him from the hands of Esau. Jacob provides us an example of what people should do when they feel fear, which is to pray. The author found an interesting statement regarding Jacob and Esau in a book titled Esau-Edom Rome by Dr. Beneyah Yashar'el.[111] "He stated in his book The Highest YAHUAH was with Jacob during this time and sent a host of angels to have supernatural encounters with Esau and his men during the night." The previous statement demonstrates how the Lord listens and responds to those who earnestly seek Him. The author did not find Dr. Yashar'el's statement in the bible but learned that he used other sources such as the Book of Jubilees. [112] "The encounters with the angels frightened Esau and his men so much that by the time they met Jacob, they were humbled and bowed to Jacob's feet, calling him lord and were willing to make peace." The intervention of angels through the dreams of Esau and his men would explain the change of heart of why they chose not to kill Jacob and make peace. The author does not believe that Esau had a complete heart change but showed kindness out of fear like Pharoah in the Book of Exodus. Each time God worked through Moses and Aaron and caused a plague upon Egypt Pharoah became fearful but shortly afterward his heart returned to its previous state. Likewise, the author believes that Esau's may have heart returned to its previous state and his descendants kept the hatred of Jacob/Israel alive.

    Esau's hatred of Jacob may have contributed to why God hates him. It should also be mentioned that Esau married two Canaanite wives and one other wife according to Genesis Chapter 36 who were Adah, Aholibamah, and Basemath. The Canaanites historically did not follow God's will to the point that Abraham and Isaac instructed their sons not to marry a Canaanite woman. Even Jesus ignored the request of a Canaanite woman in Matthew Chapter 15 until He was impressed by her great faith. Which goes to show that faith not birthright is the most essential element to the blessings of God. However, Esau/Edom historically has not shown faith and dependency upon God.

    Ironically, even though the bible clearly states God's hatred

---

[111] Esau- Edom Rome, Yashar'el, Benyah. pg. 45
[112] Esau- Edom Rome, Yashar'el, B. pg. 45-46.

for the worldly Edomites there is an exception. Individual biblical scholars believe that Job in the bible could have been an Edomite. If this is true, then God not only loved Job, but he bragged about him to Satan. Job honored God and he was faithful and obedient. Satan stated if God would take away his hedge of protection that Job would curse God to his face. Satan was allowed to affect Job's life, but he was not allowed to kill him. Job lost everything precious to him family, possessions, and his health but he never betrayed God even when he wanted to die. Through Job's endurance he was eventually rewarded double for his trouble. If Job truly is an Edomite this would be the perfect example of the grace of God and how He blesses those who are obedient and faithful to Him. That would also mean that being a descendant of Esau/Edomite is not an automatic death sentence because and Esau/Edomite can still choose to follow the Lord. Jesus Christ died and bled to save everyone who will accept Him. Furthermore, biologically Esau/Edom are not Israelites, but they are of the seed of Abraham. God blessed a multitude of people in the scriptures and claimed His prophets to righteous, but Job is the only one the scriptures not named Jesus that God bragged about. Henceforth, the author believes that Job was, and Edomite and he was supposed to belong to Satan, but he chose to serve God.

The author had a tough time finding scholarly sources to support the claim that Job was an Edomite. Two blogs Biblewise and Quora suggest that Job's father's name was Zerah or Zare who was the second son of Esau and Basemath. If what the research from the scholars of the blogs are true that would make Job, Esau's grandson, Isaac's great grandson, and Abraham's great-great grandson. Therefore, if Job is truly only five generations from Abraham he knew of the stories and great faith of Abraham and applied his personal faith the way that his great-great grandfather did. That would mean that Esau/ Edomites who choose to serve God are under the Abrahamic covenant just like Jacob/ Israelites are under the same covenant. The only difference is in the reference when the statement is made about the God of Abraham, Isaac, and Jacob because Esau is never included.

Nevertheless, God desires for all His children to return to Him but will not because they will not choose to serve Him.

People under the influence of Satan will choose the worldly ways and desires of Esau. People can learn from the example of Job regardless of their upbringing or background and choose the ways of living that please God. God was showing Satan through Job that He can penetrate the grip that Satan has over individual people that Satan thought would always be under his control. God's ways are higher than our ways and His thoughts are higher than our thoughts meaning we may never understand why God does things the way He does, but we must trust that it is for the best. Insomuch, in the authors mind it would make sense if Job were and Edomite to display God's grace and mercy upon all people.

God wants all of us to repent for our sins regardless of our genetics, race, ethnicity, or whomever we claim to be. The author believes that it is fair to say that God hates the ways of the Esau/Edomites, but He is faithful to the covenant and promises He made to the Israelites. Truth be told the author does not believe that God is pleased about the ways of the Israelites either because they behave, act, and think the ways of the Esau/Edomites. The lost and scattered tribes of Israel and Judah were cursed because of disobedience to the Most High God. The state and country of Israel was re-established by man in 1948 three years after World War II. Individual people say that God re-established Israel at this time but there has been continual conflict in that region of the world. Individual people say that man manufactured the State of Israel. In the Book of Isaiah, it refers to the Lord returning to Jerusalem and the establishment of Zion. Chapter 2 In the Book of Isaiah states that nations will no longer revolt against nation, and they will learn war no more. We know from history and current events that there is continual conflict in Israel and the Middle East. Insomuch, the author has stated that a person can be a Jew by genealogy, adoption of the faith, born into it by convert parents, or a person could be an Israelite by birth into the nation. However, it appears unlikely to the author that the above-mentioned Israelites are the same Israelites and Jews of the bible.

Minor prophets in the bible such as Obadiah, Joel, Amos, and Malachi speak of the doom of Esau. The major prophets Isaiah, Jerimiah, Ezekiel, and Daniel speak of the rath that God will place upon Edom for what they did to Israel. Esau/Edom does not miss an opportunity to make Jacob/Israel suffer. [113] "The Edomites were the sworn enemies of the children of Israel from the beginning." Even though Esau and Jacob made peace after Esau wanted to kill Jacob in The Book of Genesis, Esau's children the Edomites kept a grudge against the children of Jacob/Israelites. Today, there are various groups of different races and nationalities that claim they are the true Israelites, but nobody claims to be the true Edomites. Therefore, we must examine who might be the true Edomites.

According to the bible Esau married two Canaanite women and one Ishmaelite woman. The Canaanite women were not considered marriage material for Abrahamic men because they did not regard the Most High God. Ishmaelite women who were Semitic but were descendants of Ishmael and Hagar who were cast away from the camp of Abraham may have a grudge against the descendant of Jacob. The combination of the perceived betrayal of Jacob stealing Esau's blessing and birthright, the Canaanites disdain for the ways of God, and the casting out of Ishmael could lead to a toxic resentment towards the children of Jacob/Israel. The author believes the prementioned unions with Esau generated a generational hatred towards the people of Jacob/Israel. A strange phenomenon is the identity of modern-day Esau and Jacob is not clear. Insomuch, nobody today self identifies with Esau/Edom as people claim to be modern day Jacob/Israel.

To identify Edom history and archeology must be reviewed. [114] "Archeological sources confirm that Esau and his descendants inhabited Mount Seir amid the Horites between the years 1950 to 1926 BC." The Horites were descendants of Ham through Canaan therefore they were Canaanites. Edom and the Horites often intermarried as they lived on Mount Seir. There are stories about the Edomites that

---

[113] Hebrews to Negroes, Dalton Jr, R. pg. 314
[114] Esau- Edom Rome, Yashar'el, E. pg. 54

are varied and could lead to different theories. Nevertheless, the most convincing evidence comes from Apocrypha, specifically the Book of Jasher.

The Book of Jasher is not part of the canonized bible but it was mentioned twice once in Joshua 10:13 and secondly in 2 Samuel 1:18. Biblical scholars argue that The Book of Jasher that we have access too is different from the book the bible refers to. However, individual scholars do accept the current Book of Jasher but will say that it is not inspired writings. The Book of Jasher has various excerpts of interactions between the Israelites and Edomites. The Israelites were instructed not to fight with the Edomites. At one point Edom refused to let Israel pass through their country. [115] "For before this the lord had commanded the children of Israel saying, "You will not fight against the children of Esau" therefore the Israelites removed from them and did not fight against them." The Edomites appear to keep a grudge against the Israelites and look for ways to give them a tough time and opportunities to destroy them. However, the Edomites had conflict with another group which are the children of Chittim.

Chittim, also known as Kittim, fought against Edom under Abianus king of Chittim vs. Hadad the king of Edom. [116] "Chittim defeated Edom in battle and the children of ruled over Edom, and Edom became under the hand of the children of Chittim and became one kingdom from that day." After this battle over the years the identity of became hidden. The author believes that all people on earth are of a blended biological make-up including the mixture of Edom and Israel. However, in the blended case of Edom and Chittim individual scholars believe that Chittim is Roman.

Chittim or Kittim in the book of Genesis Chapter 10 was the son of Javan the son of Japheth the son of Noah. The sons of Javan which Kittim is along with the sons of Gomer were of the isles of the gentiles. Therefore, the (Kittim/Japheth) gentiles blended with the (Edomite/Shem) Semitic non-Israelite people and became one.

---

[115] The Complete Apocrypha, Christian Covenant Coalition pg. 444
[116] The Complete Apocrypha, Christian Covenant Coalition pg. 452

Scholars have identified that Chittim/Kittim was the modern-day island of Cyprus in the Mediterranean Sea which was once conquered by first Babylonia, then Persia, then Greece, and the Roman Empire. Edom is believed to be a war minded dominant type of people who will take over lands. Henceforth, modern Edomites could hide behind the dominant power structure of the world today.

It would be impossible to get the world to agree who are the modern day Edomites and modern-day Israelites. It is highly likely that all people have a mixture of all three of Noah's sons. However, it is evident which countries have world power and which do not. It is also evident how the leaders of the world powers look physically. That is not to say that all people who look alike think alike because the author believes that everyone has free agency to think and believe for themselves. Esau/Edom represents the world power, wealthy, dominating, controlling, warlike mindset. Jacob represents the people who trust and count on God for their redemption. The bible speaks harshly about the outcome for the Esau/Edom and how Israel/Judah will physically and spiritually be saved, spared, and redeemed as promised in the bible. Earlier in this chapter the author spoke about how he believed that Job was an example of faith and how a so-called Edomite could be blessed and spared. Nevertheless, the bible tells how the followers of Christ will be saved regardless of their origin but with a specific mandate to free and redeem the downtrodden, lost, and scattered tribes of Judah and Israel. The bible speaks about how God hates pride. God hates pride because it will keep a person from humbling themselves and repenting. Without repentance, a person is without forgiveness. Therefore, the spirit of Esau's pride and arrogance will lead to his fall.

Part Three
Identity

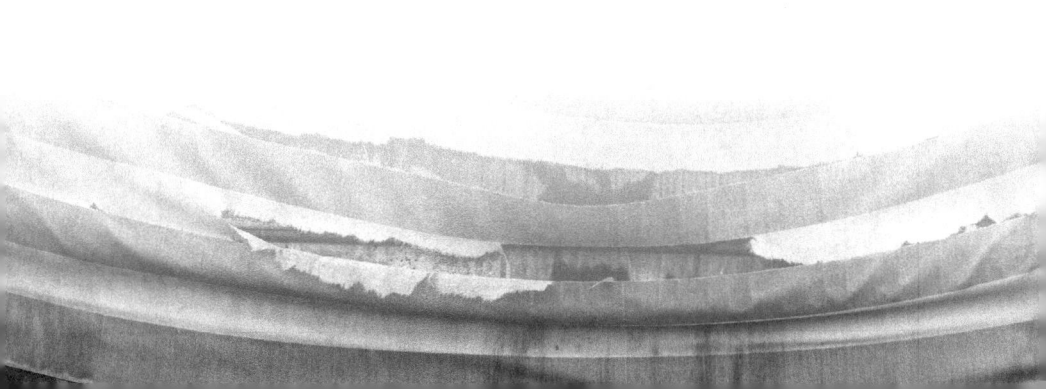

PART THREE

IDENTITY

Chapter 7
Who is Who?

Who is who from the bible in connection to who people are today is a topic that will garner a multitude of opinions, thoughts, and beliefs? Prior to stating who is who from the bible the author will address how people today compare from previous decades and generations. People today either seem narcissistic or have low self-esteem. The narcissistic person will claim remarkable things they may or may not be and the person with low self-esteem may accept whatever label or negative connotation placed upon them. The purpose of this book is not to proclaim one group of people over another but identify who people may be and bring attention to how much all people need Christ.

    In the United States black and white debates seem to be never ending. Racial relations seemed to cool off after the explosive decade of the sixty's and seemed to re-emerge during the Obama and Trump administrations. During those years there appeared to be an increase in biracial marriages and multiethnic children born. According to Pew research, in 1980 5% of the children born were biracial. That number doubled to 10% in 2000 and 14% in 2015. The same Pew research stated that 22% surveyed said that biracial children was a good thing while only 11% said that it was a terrible thing. Sixty-five percent said that biracial children did not make individuals a difference. According to a Cambridge University Press Chart only 2% of marriages were biracial and they endured public scrutiny from each side. Insomuch, we must address the differences from the past attitudes compared to now.

A modern-day researcher by the name of Dane Calloway has done significant work regarding the so-called African American indigenous people of North America which he refers to as Turtle Island. Upon watching his YouTube videos, he consistently claims that the majority of so-called African Americans did not come from Africa but are the true Negi or natives of North America. He authored a book called "Tracing Your Families Genealogical History by Records." Dane Calloway research for information by going to locations to research including using his personal finances to purchase and obtain information. Mr. Calloway's also claims that there was a paper genocide to erase evidence that that would allow so called African Americans to claim that they were here before Europeans came to the Americas. Identity in the census such as negro, mulatto, colored, black, and African American were used to distance the identity claims especially the term African American which constitutes of two different continents and would solidify the idea that people of color come from someplace else. The author finds Mr. Calloway to be a credible researcher regardless of those who oppose his claims. Nevertheless, the objective is not about Mr. Calloway but his genealogical research.

Genealogy by records can be used as proof or evidence of where people come from and to whom they are attached. Mr. Calloway challenges the records of the so- called Atlantic Slave Trade which he claims his research shows that the numbers of slaves who came from Africa were overstated and select stories about slaves were fabricated. The author will not go into details about which stories were fabricated but state that Mr. Calloway's claims have incited people and challenged others to feel uncomfortable. Insomuch, one must examine the origins of popular opinions and common beliefs.

The 1977 television series "Roots" based upon a book written by Alex Haley has stood as a standard belief of how so-called blacks came to the United States for over 40 years ago. Prior to the television series people had limited understanding, compassion, and narrow-minded personal beliefs based upon their individual upbringing. History books in public schools and libraries also played a significant role in shaping the minds of people across the world. Hollywood movies have also played a key role in shaping the minds of people about who is who. The media projection (movies, television, newspapers, magazines, and electronic medias) of people is highly influential and has lingering effects upon individual's perception of people. One aspect about entertainment and news through different media that individual people do not consider is who owns the media that shapes people's perceptions. Nothing is broadcast, printed, or downloaded without the approval of management. Over the years employees (broadcasters, reporters, and others) have become more diverse in terms of race and ethnicity but the higher-ranking management and ownership has not changed much if it all. Henceforth, the higher-ranking management and ownership in the major networks, studios, and publications is still primarily Caucasian and/or Jewish of Ashkenazi descent.

The author is not criticizing or attacking the higher-ranking management and ownership in the major networks, studios, and publications but simply stating that high-ranking management have the last word in shaping public perception. Those who have the power to influence public perception can choose to show integrity and state the facts as they are or manipulate facts to fit a story they want to portray. In the United States of America so called Asian-Americans, Hispanic Americans, Native-Americans, and African Americans have little if any say so in how they are portrayed to the public by media outlets. Each group may own individual publications or other media that is primarily marketed to and viewed by their individual group members. The group media and publications such as B. E. T. (Black Entertainment Television), Jet, and Ebony Magazines are primarily viewed by the so-called African American group but does not view the masses of people in the United States or around the world. All groups have positive and negative facts that could be said about them. However, each group of all races and ethnicities have been subjected to stereotyping and insensitive jokes.

Stereotyping throughout the years continues to shape the mindsets of people about different races and ethnicities. The 1977 television series "Roots" as mentioned in an earlier paragraph had a profound effect on a multitude of people. The concept of "Roots" consists of Alex Haley researching and tracing his genealogy back to Africa. This story solidified the idea that all so-called black people came from Africa. In the television drama so-called black Africans were helping so-called white slave catchers catch other so-called black Africans to become slaves overseas. Henceforth, one would need to ask why would an African help capture another African to be sold into slavery?

The author like others accepted this narrative without questioning why an African would help lead another African into slavery. It was rumored they betrayed their fellow Africans for money, weapons, or anything they deemed useful. The author was a child when "Roots" aired but remembers watching the series with his parents and being old enough to remember and understand what took place in the movie. The overlining belief of individual people was that so-called blacks have progressed a long way since slavery. Individual so-called blacks have excelled in sports, music, movies, and other professional fields that were less publicized. Select individuals who excelled in their fields were considered stars and exceptions of their race. However, their intellect was always considered inferior, and they lacked leadership abilities despite individuals who excelled in the medical field, law, and academia.

In January of 2018, the author learned about a Pastor named Stephen Darby of Louisville, KY who died in December of 2017. The source that the author learned about him from said that he was a powerful preacher full of the spirit and information. The author began watching his messages on YouTube and the author agreed that he was a great preacher. One of his messages was titled "Negroland." The author was intrigued by the title and watched the video. In that video he stated that negroes were not descendants of Noah's son Ham. Biblical scholars have long claimed that the children of Ham populated Africa. Pastor Darby pointed out to support his claim by using the widely accepted Zondervan Bible Dictionary which supported his claim. [117] "Ham: The youngest son of Noah, born about 96 years before the flood; and one of eight persons to live through the flood. He became the progenitor of the dark races; **not the Negros**, but the Egyptians, Ethiopians, Libyans, and Canaanites." The author had never considered anyone but Ham's descendants to have darker skin. Pastor Darby stated that the negroes were descendants of Shem and that helped the story of Joseph and his brothers not recognizing him in Egypt make sense from the Book of Genesis. Pastor Darby also showed a 1747 British map of Africa which portrayed a sub-Saharan land mass called Negroland. This map must have been hidden for years but was discovered by someone who boldly put it on the internet. The fact that it was a British map made it more convincing that it must have been legitimate. American slaves were called negroes and the derogatory slang from the word negro for years. Henceforth, Pastor Darby's video massage from Negroland opened my eyes to unthinkable possibilities.

Negroland was formed after Israelites escaped Jerusalem from the Roman invasion in 70 A.D. That means that the dark race people in that region were not African but Israelites. Therefore, in the show "Roots" Africans were not catching other Africans but Negroes who were similar in skin color but a different ethnicity. The concept about people of color coming from the line of Shem of Noah's sons never crossed the author's mind. The author was fascinated by the discovery but continued to look for more evidence. YouTube videos are far from academic credible sources therefore it is necessary to research any claims made by them. The author was amazed by the number of Caucasian and Jewish sources that support the idea that individual so-called blacks may be or are from the tribes of Israel and the tribe of Judah. A YouTuber named Dana Stevens from Chicago at the time who happens to be so-called white has been posting videos for years pleading for those who have been privileged in America to recognize that individual's judgement by the Most High God for

---

[117] Zondervan Bible Dictionary

their mistreatment of so-called black people in America. Insomuch, the overall message from brother Dana Stevens is we should treat everybody with love and kindness regardless of their skin color but those who continue mistreatment of people of color will have to answer to God.

The author wants to go overboard to make it clear that all people matter to God. Also, to remind people of John 3:16 that God so loved the world that He gave His Only Begotten Son that we all shall live by accepting Jesus Christ as our Lord and Savior. The Apostle Paul who was a Benjamite from the Tribe if Israel intentionally preached the Gospel of Jesus Christ to the gentiles knowing that those who accepted the gospel would continue to spread the good news. Paul did a great deal of teaching and preaching in Turkey and Greece (Europe) as they received the gospel better than his own people. Those who fully accept the gospel of Jesus Christ will be saved and that does not have anything to do with race or ethnicity. However, individual people do not know who they are or where they came from, which is the main purpose of this book.

The purpose of this book is for identity purposes mainly and for people to wake up to the truth and stop mistreating people based upon race and ethnicity. We should all be brothers and sisters in Christ. In the bible Matthew 19:30, Mark 10:31, and Luke 13:30 say that the last shall be first and the first shall be last. The author believes this is referring to the status of people in the world. In every industrialized nation as a whole people of color are considered lowest in status. In general, you do not see people of color in high-ranking political positions. It was not until the 2008 presidential election that the United States elected Barak Obama to the highest office. Often overlooked is President Obama ancestry was of mixed or blended genealogy because his skin is browner than tan. Individual people of color have flourished in the United States but are often treated as an exception or a credit to their race. In other industrialized nations all their leaders have the same complexion and people of color who reside there are often unseen and unheard. In North America in the country of Mexico people have varying skin tones but the leaders are often lighter in complexion. In Matthew 19:30 it states individuals that are first shall be last meaning that all who are first do not have to be last. The author believes those who are first and accept Jesus Christ as their Lord and Savior and live accordingly to the scriptures do not have to fall. God is not a respecter of persons and He made all of us, so our skin color has nothing to do with our salvation. Therefore, it is mankind that made the stigma of skin color become an issue not God.

If skin color is not an issue for God, then why is it for man? The author believes that individual people want to feel superior to others because it increases their self-worth. However, for one to be superior to another must be perceived as inferior therefore that person's self-worth is lower than it should be. People who experience love and know their family history are more secure about their self-worth. However, those people who do not experience love or have limited knowledge about their family struggle with an identity crisis.

The so-called African American are the only group of people identified by two continents and not a country. So called Asian Americans know if they are Chinese, Japanese, Korean, Filipino, or other countries in Asia. Hispanic or Latino Americans know if they are Mexican, Puerto Rican, Jamaican, Dominican, Haitian, Cuban or other countries. So called white Americans do not identify as European American but American however they know if they are German, Polish, English, French, Irish, Italian, or any other European country. People who come from Africa to visit or live know if they are Nigerian, Ghanese, Egyptian, Sudanese, Ethiopian, Kenyan, or any other African country. The same is true for anyone from the so-called Middle Eastern Countries. The lack of identity made Stephen Darby's message on the 1747 English map of Negroland so intriguing. It gave a location for the American Negro. However, someone decided to hide the map and tried to erase it from history. The continent of Africa was later divided by European powers, boundaries were changed, and individual countries were renamed as Negroland no longer existed. The so-called negro no longer wanted to be called a negro because of the negative and derogatory remarks associated with it. The terms "black" and "African American" were adapted in place of negro to become politically correct. Insomuch, losing the term negro disconnected the people in America from a particular region in Africa that would potentially connect them to people who were Hebrew and from the lineage of Shem and the lineage of Judah or Israel.'

Rudolph Windsor authored a book called "From Babylon to Timbuktu" which spoke about a history of ancient so-called black races including black Hebrews. Another academic researcher Ivan Sertima who was an Associate Professor at Rutgers University authored a book titled "They Came Before Columbus" which had documented voyages across the Atlantic Ocean from West Africa long before Christopher Columbus discovered a land that was already occupied by people to claim as his own. That would help support Dane Calloway's belief that so-called black people were already on the American continent prior to Christopher Columbus and the Atlantic Slave Trade. However, it was information that was found in the Church of Jesus Christ of Latter-Day Saints' Book of Mormon that was found most interesting that would place Hebrews from the line of Joseph of the Tribe of Israel in the Americas around 600 B.C.

Part Four

Book of Mormon
(The Church of Jesus Christ of Latter-Day Saints)

Chapter 8

Overview of The Church of Jesus Christ of Latter-Day Saints

The Church of Jesus Christ of Latter- Day Saints was founded by Joseph Smith in 1830. According to church records there are over 16.6 million members on record in 2020. The church is led by a president who is prophet, seer, revelator, and who holds all the keys to the priesthood. He has two counselors and a Quorum of Twelve as his direct supporters and additional leadership. There is also a Quorum of Seventy that preside over different areas of the country and world who provide guidance stake area (stake) and local (individual) churches. All men who are in the church are the patriarchs of their families and have either the Levitical or Melchizadek priesthood. The church is family oriented, and the women are respected, and children are considered a blessing. Henceforth, the church focus is Christ centered and dedicated to spreading the gospel.

The Church of Jesus Christ of Latter-Day Saints believes in the Father, the Son, and The Holy Ghost as the Godhead three in one purpose. Nevertheless, the church has not been accepted as Christian by select so-called mainstream Christians because of theological differences and The Book of Mormon which no other religion or denomination uses. The early Latter-Day Saint Church "Mormons" were often ridiculed and persecuted by local people which led to them being chased out of towns. The Church Head

Quarters began in Palmyra, NY to Kirtland, OH, Independence, MO, Nauvoo, IL, Winter Quarters, NE, and finally settled in Salt Lake City, UT. Today the church has wards (individual churches) and stakes (regions/districts) in every state in America. The church has members in over 160 countries and has 267 temples in over sixty different countries. Insomuch, it must be stated for "The Church of Jesus Christ of Latter-Day Saints" the churches and temples are two entirely different things.

The church buildings are the Sunday meeting places and the temples are special meeting places to do ordinances such as Baptism for the Dead, Endowments, Initiatory, and sealings of marriages and families. The Sunday Meetings consist of the Sacrament Meetings where you have prayer, songs, announcements, speakers with spiritual messages, and the Sacrament (Communion) bread and water/wine. There are also Sunday School Sessions, High Priesthood, Elders Quorum, Relief Society (Women), and Age Group sessions for children with a Nursery for the young children. The church is extremely family oriented and places immense value on the roles of family life. The church is socially conservative by nature and is usually extremely helpful to members, neighbors, and co-workers. The men and women in the church have a reputation for being hard and honest workers in which there are high-ranking professionals such as doctors, engineers, lawyers, businessmen, teachers, and so-forth people who would be considered positive members of society. Nevertheless, individual members of society refuse to embrace Latter Day Saints or so-called Mormons as Christian.

The two main criticisms against the church by mainstream Christians and society was polygamy marriages and the exclusion of so-called blacks from the priesthood. The first issue of discussion is polygamy. In 1890 the Latter-Day Saint Church officially stopped having plural marriages. The church claimed to have a revelation about ending polygamy. On September 25, 1890, Church President Woodruff announced the Manifesto which on paper to end the practice of plural marriages being accepted by the church. The congress of the United States increased its attention to uphold anti-polygamy laws by disincorporate the church which would cost the church substantial money to lose their tax-exempt status and slow down the churches ability to build new temples. The current members in plural marriages did not dissolve but individual members produced creative living arrangements. There were other sects of the church that did not discontinue the practice of polygamy, but they were not part of the largest branch based out of Salt Lake City, Utah. Individual people confuse the sects that still practice polygamy today with the largest branch of the church. Henceforth, there are details the author could discuss about polygamy in the church, but they would detract from the main purpose of this book.

The second popular issue with the church is the Black Priesthood Ban. So- called black men were not initially banned from having the priesthood in the church. Joseph Smith the founder of the church ordained a man named Elijah Abel and others to the priesthood. The author believes that a man named William McCrary outraged Brigham Young and caused the decision. McCrary was considered half black and half Indian. McCrary was baptized and later ordained to the priesthood. However, McCrary began claiming that he was a prophet and possessed supernatural gifts. He appeared crazy to people and even claimed that he was Adam from the bible. He was excommunicated in 1847 for apostacy. After his excommunication he continued preaching and began to attract followers from the Latter-Day Saint Church and to make matters worse he began sealing marriages to so-called white women. This infuriated the members of the church and especially Brigham Young. However, it was Parley Pratt, an Apostle of the church who made the first statement about skin color being an issue and said that descendants of Ham were cursed from the priesthood.

One must consider the time that the church began in 1830. Slavery was legal and so-called blacks did not have much if any rights including freed slaves. Individual Latter-Day Saints took slaves with them to Utah. Women also had few if any rights and all policies were set by so-called white men without any outside influences.

Nevertheless, any form of bigotry, supremacy, or domination has never been acceptable in the eyes of God.

Latter Day Saints were trailblazers and very progressive for their days. No church that was primarily Caucasian was accepting black members and let alone giving them leadership responsibilities opportunities such as the priesthood. Elijah Abel and others were praised for their service and dedication, but the author does not believe they were ever seen as equal to their so-called white counterparts. Joseph Smith the founder of the church died in 1844 while the official ban of blacks from the priesthood did not take place until 1852. The McCrary excommunication did not take place until 1847 meaning that blacks were allowed to have the priesthood during Joseph Smith's entire reign as president of the church. It was during Brigham Young's reign as church president that McCrary's antics infuriated the leadership of the church that lead to the ban. The church has a long-standing habit of being a respecter of persons and showing blind obedience to the leadership of the church. The priesthood ban was never God ordained but it played upon the fear of the possibility of so-called black men marrying and cohabitating with so-called white females and have equal authority with them. Insomuch, wild excuses such as the curse of Ham and the curse of Cain became common place for priesthood denial in the early church.

The perceived Curse of Ham is a biblical misrepresentation because the bible clearly states that Noah cursed Canaan the son of Ham. Ham had three other sons who were not cursed. Ham was blessed with Noah and his two brothers by God therefore there was never a curse on Ham. Secondly, the curse place upon Cain in the bible was that he would be a fugitive and vagabond upon the earth. He received a mark so people would not kill him. A mark is usually relatively small located somewhere upon a person and typically not a whole body covering. Furthermore, all the descendants of Cain died in the flood. The wives of Noah's sons were sisters according to the Book of Jubilees and were actual cousins of Noah and was not from the lineage of Cain. A third popular excuse was that so-called black people were less valiant in the premortal life prior to coming to earth. Apostle Bruce R. McConkie publicly spoke about the blacks were less valiant without any scriptural support or any other support. [118] "Those who were less valiant in pre-existence and thereby had certain restrictions imposed upon them during mortality and are known to us as negroes." McConkie's statements are difficult to conceive that a high-ranking official could make such a claim. The belief of so-called blacks not being valiant, worthy, or eligible to receive the priesthood had been around for years prior to McConkie's statement and unfortunately individual so-called Mormons believed and accepted the racial biases as the truth. The church had other negative beliefs about relations with so-called black people that will be discussed more in a different section of the book. However, it must be noted that despite the negative mindset towards the reasons for the priesthood ban there are not any recorded episodes of violence or mistreatment of people of color by Latter-Day Saints.

On June 1, 1978, Latter Day Saint President Spencer W. Kimball announced the Official Decoration 2 which stated that all were alike to God including black and white, bond and free, male, and female. The declaration allowed men of color to receive the priesthood. The ban of so-called blacks from the priesthood lasted over 120 years in 1978 however the church never had official doctrine to substantiate the ban. The church presented the declaration as a revelation from God. The Lord does correct those He loves and when His children do not listen to the Spirit, He has a way of correcting in ways that are not understood by men. God's timetable is different from men therefore generations could pass before their correction takes place. However, there are individuals who would argue that the lifting of the ban was due to pressure from the government to take away their tax-exempt status.

The church has received criticism, controversy, and persecution since the early days of the church. Regardless of the negativity the church has faced they have stood strong. The author has associated

---

[118] Mormon Doctrine, p 527, 1966 ed.

with individual members of the church over 30 years and must testify that individual Latter Day Saints are the nicest and hardest working people that he ever met. Most active members are zealous for good works and eager to serve God in the name of Jesus Christ. The problem that most non-Latter-Day Saints have with the church is the doctrine, specifically the Book of Mormon. Non-members believe they have their own bible. The truth is the church uses the King James Version Bible and the Book of Mormon which is another testament of Jesus Christ. Members who were born into the church or multi-generational members of the church seem to value the Book of Mormon over the bible. The church has a writing called the 13 Articles of Faith which states: [119] "We believe the Bible to be the word of God as far as it is translated correctly; we also believe the Book of Mormon to be the word of God." The members believe that the Book of Mormon has less translation flaws and value it more for accuracy. Individual converts to the church seem to value the bible over the Book of Mormon because of their history of only knowing the bible. The author was raised in a Baptist Church that read the King James Version Bible. Upon the author meeting his future wife he never met or at least knew any people who were Latter Day Saints or at that time so-called Mormons. Henceforth, as the author got to know his future wife and family a positive perspective of so-called Mormons was developed.

    The author had selected doctrinal issues with the church because they seemed strange and foreign to him. Baptism for the Dead, Celestial Marriage, and Second Nephi Chapter 5 verse twenty-one were the three key issues for the author. At the time the priesthood ban, and polygamy was no longer an issue for the church. The attitude of the author regarding the Church of Jesus Christ of Latter-Day Saints and The Book of Mormon was if the topic or similar scripture can be found in the bible then the author could accept it. The author always believed that there was more to the scriptures than the eye could see in the bible. When the author received the

---

[119] Pearl of Great Price

Book of Mormon, Doctrines and Covenants, and the Pearl of Great Price he was intrigued because he found more scriptural types of writings. However, it was not until the author enrolled in the Colorado Theological Seminary Class GBNT 638 Exposing the Devil's Liar that he discovered during research the Book of Enoch, Book of Jubilees, Book of Jasher, and other Apocrypha books.

The discovery of other scriptures that did not conflict with the bible but helped explain select missing details of scripture was fascinating to the author. That also meant that the Church of Jesus Christ of Latter-Day Saints did not have a monopoly of books that complimented and supported the bible. The author began to question everything, not just the LDS Church but all religious practices but he never questioned his belief in God or salvation. The author was an active member of the church for over 15 years before becoming inactive. The author and his wife took two different one-year journeys visiting other churches of various faiths. However, they eventually returned to worship with the church.

The author discovered during the yearlong visitations of different denominations that most churches are fundamentally similar, rooted in Christ but have individual variations in theological beliefs and practices. All churches have their own positive aspects, quirks, and imperfections which is how all people are. No person or church is perfect, but God is perfect. People and churches are addicted to wanting to be right, the most correct, and being the person or church that God loves the most. Satan goes to church too and he knows how people work so he will use information to cause division and strife among believers. Individual churches claim to be the one true church. When people or churches make that statement, you are inadvertently saying that other churches are false. God wants to know from all people if we accept Jesus Christ as our Lord and Savior. If people accept Jesus Christ as their Lord and Savior and that He rose from the dead, then you are part of His church. If you do not believe that Jesus Christ rose from the dead, then you are an antichrist. [120] "Who

---

[120] 1 John 2:22 (KJV)

is a liar but he that denieth that Jesus is the Christ? He is antichrist, that denieth the Father and the Son." The Church of Jesus Christ of Latter-Day Saints also points out that there are just two sides in the Book of 1 Nephi. [121] "And he said unto me: Behold there are save two churches only; the one is the church of the Lamb of God, and the other is the church of the devil; wherefore, whoso belongeth not to the church of the Lamb of God belongeth to that great church, which is the mother of abominations; and she is the whore of all the earth." People in kindness ask other people what church do you go to (denominationally)? A better question would be do you believe in Christ. There are good and decent people who have not chosen Christ yet for a variety of reasons or excuses and are unknowingly defaulting to the opposite of Christ's church. Therefore, if you choose Jesus and believe Him you are part of God's church but if you do not choose or reject God you are part of the devil's church.

The name of the church "The Church of Jesus Christ of Latter-Day Saints" tells you who they serve. It is not called the church of Joseph Smith or Brigham Young. The author believes that the church has been guilty of human frailties and was criticized publicly. God corrects all his servants. The pride of wanting to be correct, the best, most loved, or most holy can lead people to put others down to magnify self. The author believes that the church is finally putting aside pride and moving in the right direction. The church has been telling its members to distance themselves from using the nickname Mormon. Select theology displayed by what was called the Mormon Church has been bizarre, sexist, and racist and does not apply to the standards and beliefs that the Church of Jesus Christ is displaying today. Furthermore, so-called Mormons have been viewed as a cult by various people. However, the term cult is used loosely because it is easy to label a group a cult because they have beliefs that are different from your own.

Warren Jeffs was the leader of the Fundamentalists Church of Jesus Christ of Latter-Day Saints (FLDS) who was convicted of

---

[121] 1 Nephi 1:14 Book of Mormon

sexually abusing underage girls. Jeffs is serving a life sentence but somehow still maintains a degree of control over his diminished following. The FLDS church broke away from the church when they announced that polygamy was no longer a doctrine of the church. When the church practiced polygamy, it violated what was written in the third book of The Book of Mormon called Jacob. [122] "Wherefore, my brethren, hear me, and hearken to the word of the Lord: For there shall not any man among you have save it be one wife; and concubines he shall have none;." Warren Jeffs could be considered a cult leader because his law is above God's law. Joseph Smith, Brigham Young, and other initial church leaders were guilty of trying to justify themselves because David, Solomon, Abraham, and Jacob had multiple wives in the churches Doctrines and Covenants but that was never God's will. There are other sects of the original Church of Jesus Christ, but the largest branch has been corrected to align with scriptures.

The author believes that The Church of Jesus Christ is Christian despite its public scrutiny for being different and called a cult by so-called mainstream Christianity. The author is not Mormon, but he is becoming a saint in the latter days. All churches that claim that Jesus Christ as Lord and Savior and strive to live by the scriptures the author supports. Henceforth, the author supports the current leadership of the Latter-Day Saints.

---

[122] Jacob 2:27 Book of Mormon

Chapter 9
Connection to Biblical Genealogy

The Book of Mormon begins with a chapter called 1 Nephi which tells a story of a family led by a man named Lehi and his wife Sariah who had four sons named Laman, Lemuel, Sam, and Nephi. This family is Jewish as the father Lehi was warned in a dream to leave Jerusalem to spare his life. Individual stories in the Book of Mormon give account to the history and descendants of this family that left Jerusalem and sailed to the Americas. Henceforth, their history and accounts would not be documented anywhere in Asia, Europe, or Africa because they were not considered a prominent family during their time in Jerusalem.

The youngest son Nephi was considered a righteous man who served the Lord. He was the person who kept the historical records of events as well as a member of his descendants after him. The first book in the Book of Mormon is 1 Nephi and in chapter 6 Nephi stated that he does not focus on the genealogy of his fathers. However, he did give significant information. [123] "For it suffices me to say that we are descendants of Joseph." The author believes that he is speaking of the favorite son of Jacob/Israel the boy with the coat of colors. Henceforth, we lack the genealogy from Joseph to Lehi and Nephi, but we have the genealogy of Joseph and prior in the bible.

Assuming that Joseph is the same son of Jacob/Israel there is a

---

[123] 1 Nephi 6: 2 Book of Mormon

biblical connection, however we do not know if Lehi and Nephi come through the lines of Manasseh or Ephraim. Regardless, this would make the descendants of Lehi and Nephi Hebrew and under the covenant of Abraham, Isaac, and Jacob in the bible. 1 Nephi also informs us that the wives of the sons come from the descendants of Ishmael. The bible informs us that Ishmael comes from the union between the Patriarch Abraham and Hagar who was his wife Sarah's handmaid. The bible tells us that Hagar was Egyptian which means she descended from Mizraim the son of Ham the son of Noah. The children of Ham were credited with populating the modern-day continent of Africa as proclaimed by the Book of Jubilees. Insomuch, assumptions can be made about the physical appearance of the children of Ishmael and its Egyptian ties from Abraham, Isaac, and Jacob's timeline inn history.

The physical appearance of Egyptians based upon the cave and pyramid paintings dated in ancient times depicts skin tones ranging from tan to deep brown hues. Brown appears to be the dominant color of people based upon photographs of artwork dated ancient times. Though skin color has nothing to do with salvation the author is using the premises of skin color to identify a group of people based upon biblical, historical, and archeological information available to us at this time. Let us also consider Joseph and his wife Asenath who is mentioned in the bible twice in the Book of Genesis. [124] "And Pharaoh called Joseph's name Zaphnathpaaneah; and he gave him to wife Asenath the daughter of Potipherah priest of On." And Joseph went out over all the land of Egypt. Therefore, Asenath like Hagar before her was an Egyptian woman and had skin of a brownish hue. Joseph righteousness and spiritual gifts promoted by Pharoah to be the second highest ranking person in Egypt. He had authority over the food sources in all the land of Egypt. When famine was spread across the globe the children of Israel were informed that Egypt had food, so Israel sent his oldest sons to Egypt to gather food. After their arrival in Egypt, they came across their long-lost

---

[124] Genesis 41:45 (KJV)

brother Joseph who recognized them immediately, but they did not recognize him. [125] "And Joseph knew his brethren, but they knew not him." This meant that Joseph looked like an Egyptian in clothing and physical appearance. The brothers assumed that their brother was either dead or that they would never see him again, so they did not consider looking for him. Nevertheless, if Israelite or Jews had the physical appearance of the Israelites and Jews that we are familiar with today Joseph would have stood out and been obvious he was not an Egyptian. Joseph would have been recognized by his brothers as either a ghost, doppelganger, or their long-lost brother.

The fact that Joseph's brothers could not identify him suggest that Egyptians and Hebrews has similar skin hues. That ideology would also suggest that Hebrews had tan to deep brown skin tones like the Egyptians which also meant they were distinguished by clothing and language. Today most Egyptians in leadership are lighter in skin tone primarily tan. One must consider today that considerable time has passed since the invasions of Greece and Rome who intermingled with the Egyptians and lighten the complexion of their offspring. The Church of Jesus Christ of Latter-Day Saints has various beautiful artworks on the walls of the church that depicts the descendants of Lehi's youngest son Nephi (Nephites) as having so-called white skin and his oldest son Laman (Lamanites) as having tan to light brown skin. However, despite the beauty of the artwork, the descendants of Joseph and his wife Asenath that both the Nephites and Lamanites likely had brownish skin.

The author does not have an interest for the church to change all their paintings to be historically accurate regarding skin tone since the Gospel of Jesus Christ and His Salvation is preached. The author must also reiterate that he does not have an agenda to make all significant scriptural figures brown or so-called black. None of the people living today can conclusively know or prove anything because we were not living in those times. The author is gathering the available information from scriptures, history, and archeology

---

[125] Genesis 42:8 (KJV)

and piecing together likely possibilities that were either overlooked or ignored. Henceforth, the author is challenging conventional thinking about the identity and features of people to considered based upon available information and developing a theology.

The "World History Chart" in accordance with Bible Chronology is a circular thirty-seven" x 45" poster chart with dates and times of history and bible events that happened simultaneously. The author found the chart to be amazing by itself, henceforth by chance he checked the date and claims of the Book of Mormon arrival to the Americas. The placement of Native Americans in the Americas lines up with the Book of Mormon timeline when they escaped Jerusalem and the overcoming of King Nebuchadnezzar. The Book of Mormon 1 Nephi Chapter 18 states that the family finished constructed a boat and set sail to their promised land. The perceived promised land is what would become known as the American Continents. Information is not available about how long it took to build the boat, how long it took to sail across the seas, or what route they took. Scholars who doubt the authenticity of the Book of Mormon disregard all its contents, those who accept the contents of The Book of Mormon speculate on the route to the Americas and landing locations. The author does not claim that all South American cultures came from the family in the Book of Mormon. Based upon the ancient remains from the Inca, Mayan, Olmec, and Aztec cultures there is evidence of African and Asian influence in the sculptures, cave art, and architecture. Insomuch, based upon the historical documents and relative scriptures one can only develop theories based upon limited resources.

Supposing the Book of Mormon information is true that would establish a Sematic connection from the south upwards to Central and North America. In the book "They Came Before Columbus" by Ivan Van Sertima talked about West African mariners sailing to the America's hundreds of years before Christopher Columbus claimed to discover America. Other scholars have agreed that individual Indian Tribes crossed over from Asia to the Americas through the Bearing Strait and travelled southward. Both routes could stem from the invasion of Babylon to the countries of Israel and Judah. The scattering of Israel from the north through the Bearing Straight could include mixing with Asian people an altering the appearance of how they looked in Israel or captivity in Babylon. Likewise, individual scholars believe those who escaped to the south of Israel and Judah through Egypt, other parts of Africa have altered their physical characteristics though intermingling.

Regardless of the physical characteristics of people the most essential element is connection to the spiritual kingdom. God made a covenant with a group of people who disobeyed him, they were scattered across the globe not knowing who they were. Jesus said in the New Testament that He was come to gather the lost sheep of Israel. However, in the process His salvation became open to all people who accept Him. The Book of Mormon shows ties to the lost sheep of Israel hidden on the other side of thew world to the third and fourth corners North and South America. The spreading across the earth confirms the prophecy in the bible. [126] "And he shall set up an ensign for the nations, and shall assemble the outcasts of Israel, and gather the dispersed of Judah from the four corners of the earth." Isaiah spoke about the scattered as outcasts in the nations of the world. Nobody is more outcast upon industrialized nations than so-called Black people. In the United States during the early to mid-20th century Hollywood consistently portrayed so-called Black people and so-called Indians as the lowest forms of humanity as either being animalistic, violent, lazy, and lacking intelligence. Henceforth, the perception of so-called black people which would also include other people of color such as the so-called Indians was/has been negative for a long time.

The families in The Book of Mormon primarily the Nephites and Lamanites were constantly warring with each other. When you read the Book of Mormon without discernment you will assume that the Lamanites are dark skinned and evil, and Nephites are white skinned and righteous. Nevertheless, the Book of Mormons

---

[126] Isaiah 11:12 (KJV)

mentions a time when the Lamanites were more righteous than the Nephites. The Bible and The Book of Mormon make it clear that righteousness comes from the grace bestowed upon us from our Lord and Savior. In the author's opinion the bible is the source of direction for spiritual righteousness. The Book of Mormon is a supplementary book that supports the bible, and its people (Nephites and Lamanites) connected to the bible as offspring of Joseph the son of Jacob/Israel.

CHAPTER 10

BOOK OF MORMON PERCEIVED REFERENCES TO SKIN COLOR

This chapter is not an attempt to belittle, embarrass, or disgrace The Church of Jesus Christ of Latter-Day Saints however select material presented in this chapter will not show favorable regarding the attitudes and beliefs of individual church leaders of the past. The current and modern members of the church the author has associated with have never shown outward attitudes and beliefs of racism and prejudice in the authors presence. However, individual members who grew up in the church prior to the 1978 removal of the priesthood ban appear to try to conceal preconceived thoughts or beliefs about people of color. Most members were successful at concealing any previous racist attitudes towards people of color while individuals may have disagreed with racism prior to 1978. Nevertheless, the church cannot deny that there were racists beliefs among individuals in the leadership of the church in the past. Insomuch, there were multiple things believed and published in Mormon publications that were racist.

    The first place to start is in the Book of Mormon 2 Nephi 5:21 which was initially a red flag to a bible believer and citizen of the United States of America. [127] "And he had caused the cursing to come upon them, yea, even a sore cursing, because of their iniquity. For behold, they had hardened their hearts against him, that they

---

[127] 1 Nephi 5:21 Book of Mormon

had become like unto a flint; wherefore, as they were white, and exceedingly fair and, delightsome that they might not be enticing unto my people the Lord God did cause a skin of blackness to come upon them." When the author read this with a carnal mind the versed screamed racist because it implied that the Lord cursed people with black skin because of their sin. The verse also implied that white skin was better, righteous, beautiful, and pleasing to the Lord. It would be easy to see how the carnal mind of anyone who read this verse especially those who had white skin would feel superior to those who did not have the same skin. Also consider that during the conception of the discovery of The Book of Mormon that slavery was legal and people of color including the so-called Indians did not have any rights in the United States. The only people who truly had any rights in the 1800s in the United States were so-called white males. However, there is a spiritual aspect to 2 Nephi 5:21.

Spiritually speaking 2 Nephi 5:21 was talking about the behavior of those who chose not to follow God and it was their spirit that became hard like unto flint. The white they refer to in the book is light and the skin of blackness is spiritual darkness. If God cuts off a person His light is unable to flow through that person therefore, they are in darkness because they do not have the spirit of God in them. The bible has a variety of verses referring to spiritual light and spiritual darkness. [128] "Then spake Jesus again unto them, saying, I am the light of the world: he that followeth me shall not walk in darkness, but shall have the light of life." The previous verse refers to what Jesus said about light and darkness of the spirit. The bible never refers to a man's skin changing because of sin. In the Book of Jeremiah, the bible talks about a man's skin becoming dark because of the heat of the sun and due to famine but never sin. However, in the Book of Leviticus talks about a man's skin turning white as snow and calling it leprosy. Henceforth, bible readers rarely acknowledge there are clean forms of leprosy such as freckles, hair loss, and pigment loss known today as vitiligo.

---

[128] John 8:12 (KJV)

The bible gives two distinct times when people's skin turned white as snow because of sin in The Book of 2 Kings chapter 5 and The Book of Numbers Chapter 12. Gehazi lied and was deceitful seeking riches and personal gain in 2 Kings caught in his lie and sin by the prophet Elisha. Gehazi received the curse of leprosy (Naaman's Leprosy) of being white as snow that would cling to his family forever. Often overlooked from the previous scripture is the word forever. That means that Gehazi's descendants are still on earth today and will continue in the future. The way the verse is written Gehazi was punished for his deceit and cursed with skin as white as snow because of his wicked choice. The author doubts that Gehazi had gross leprosy with excessive growths on the skin or disfigures the body because nobody would desire to marry or have children with his descendants. Miriam the sister of Moses murmured about her brother Moses to her other brother Aaron about Moses choice of wife and God heard it and she received a curse of the skin of leprosy as white as snow. Moses was not cursed with leprosy, but the Lord told him to put his hand to his bosom and his hand became leprous as white as snow and when he removed his hand it was restored like his other hand which was not white as snow. If the Book of Mormon is truly another testament of Jesus Christ, then it would not conflict with the Bible but support it. Therefore, to support the bible then 2 Nephi must be talking about spiritual darkness/blackness and not the physical outward blackness of the skin.

The author believes the early leaders of The Church of Jesus Christ of Latter- Day Saints must have interpreted 2 Nephi 5:21 meaning the outward skin of a person or else they would not have made public statements that were published in church sponsored articles. The second president of the church Brigham Young made multiple statements about black skin that are perceived as racist without scriptural support. [129] "Brigham Young taught a much greater extreme. In a sermon given on March 8, 1863, Young stated, "Shall I tell you the law of God in regard to the African race? *If the*

---

[129] Journal of Discourses, 10:110

white man who belongs to the chosen seed mixes his blood with the seed of Cain, the penalty, under the law of God, is death on the spot. This will always be so (*Journal of Discourses*, 10:110)." Either people of African ancestry are not of the seed of Cain or Brigham Young had a false prophecy on this issue because there have been multitudes of mixed child conceptions since 1863 so there should have been a multitude of people who died on the spot. The author believes this was a scare tactic to keep members from intermingling with so-called black people and not a revelation from God. Noteworthy, Brigham Young position as president and prophet of the church made him an easy target as an example of a racist based on select comments.

Brigham Young was noted in Chapter 8 of this book as having a conflict with so-called black member and priesthood holder named Pete McCrary for his wild claims and marrying so called white women. [130] "According to Brigham Young, Joseph Smith classified these people as *The Seed of Cain*. Young said that "Joseph Smith had declared that the Negroes were not neutral in heaven, for all the spirits took sides, but 'the posterity of Cain are black because he (Cain) committed murder. He killed Abel and God set a mark upon his posterity *(The Way to Perfection*, Joseph Fielding Smith, p.105)." The church has a long history of being respecter of persons especially by titles, and never questioning what a leader says. However, when Brigham Young led the saints out to Utah there were few that would challenge his authority. Furthermore, the previous statement about the negro not being neutral in heaven shows an air of racial supremacy. How could anybody know about the neutrality or lack thereof in heaven? The church began a history of excommunicating members who challenged authority even if you were one of the Three Witness to the Book of Mormon authenticity. The author perceived that the threat of excommunication became a scare tactic to keep members from challenging the authority of their leaders. The author can imagine members thinking select statements were outrageous but went with the flow anyway. One of the problems

---

[130] The Way to Perfection p. 105

with the seed of Cain claim is that Brigham Young put the blame on Joseph Smith and claimed that he endorsed this belief after Joseph Smith was murdered and could not speak for himself. The author believes Brigham Young knew that nobody would have the nerve to rebuttal the martyred prophet of the church. However, there is another serious flaw to Brigham Young's claim about Negroes being the seed of Cain was that Cain's seed were wiped out in the flood of Noah.

The author researched the genealogy of Noah and his sons which the bible supports that Noah and his sons all trace back to Adam and Eve through Seth. The genealogy of Cain is mentioned in the Book of Genesis but is incomplete. According to the Apocrypha Book of Jubilees the wives of Noah's sons were sisters, and they were cousins of Noah. Therefore, wives of Noah's sons were not from the seed of Cain. Biblical scholars claim that Ham's descendants populated the continent known as Africa and the darker race people. The author believes that to keep the purity of the so-called white race that it was necessary to demonize the so-called black race through Ham's wife and making her the link to dark skinned people. [131]"And after the flood we are told that the curse that had been pronounced upon Cain was continued through Ham's wife, as he had married a wife of that seed. And why did it pass through the flood? *Because it was necessary that the devil should have a representation upon the earth as well as God*" (Journal of Discourses 22:304)." The question should have been asked who told them of the false story of Ham's wife carrying the seed of Cain. They said the devil should have representation on earth through dark skinned people from Ham's wife. The article shows that the leaders of the day interpreted 2 Nephi 5:21 as literally being a curse of black skin. Unfortunately, the stories regarding black skin continued from the 1800s to 1978.

The main problem with the interpretation of dark or black skin by the early church leaders that it is not supported by the Bible, The Book of Mormon, or another document "The Pearl of Great Price."

---

[131] Journal of Discourses 22:304

Man's interpretation can misconstrue or manipulate scriptures to mean what they want it to mean for personal agendas. The author is not claiming that early church leaders were hateful or malicious but stating they were a product of their environment born at a time that racial superiority was the norm. [132] "Tenth LDS President Joseph Fielding Smith wrote, "It was well understood by the early elders of the Church that the mark which was placed on Cain and which his posterity inherited was the black skin." The Book of Moses inside "The Pearl of Great Price" informs us that Cain and his descendants were black" (*The Way to Perfection*, p.107). Years after Brigham Young the church held to theory of so-called black people descending from Cain. [133] "Joseph Fielding Smith also stated that "there is a reason why one man is born black and with other disadvantages, while another is born white with great advantages. The reason is that we once had an estate before we came here, and were obedient; more or less, to the laws. Those who were faithful in all things there received greater blessings here, and those who were not faithful received less" (*Doctrines of Salvation* 1:61)." The mindset of men was common among all people for years. Individual so-called black people felt inferior and disadvantaged without a known cause other that being told they were black. The Civil Rights Movement did gain strength during the 1950s and 60s. Henceforth, the era created individual so-called black influential leaders who began to build self-esteem in the black community while disrupting or agitating the beliefs of so-called white people.

Select beliefs about dark or black skin in the church and in America still existed in the 1960s. [134] "For these reasons, Bruce McConkie would write, "The negroes are not equal with other races where the receipt of certain spiritual blessings is concerned, particularly the priesthood and the temple blessings that flow therefrom..." (*Mormon Doctrine*, p.527, 1966 ed.)." The spirits of those

---

[132] The Way to Perfection, p. 107
[133] Doctrines of Salvation 1:61
[134] Mormon Doctrine, p. 527, 1966 ed.

with dark or black skin were perceived as less valiant. [135] "According to LDS Apostle Bruce McConkie, those who fought on God's side "were more valiant than others...Those who were less valiant in pre-existence and who thereby had certain spiritual restrictions imposed upon them during mortality are known to us as the negroes. Such spirits are sent to earth through the lineage of Cain, the mark put upon him for his rebellion against God and his murder of Abel being a black skin...The present status of the negro rests purely and simply on the foundation of pre-existence" (*Mormon Doctrine*, p.527, 1966 ed.)." Bruce McConkie was referring to the battle in heaven when Satan and his angels fought in heaven against God's angels. The author does not know if McConkie's statement came from a so-called revelation, doctrine of men, or hidden scripture by which he was unable to identify a source of its authenticity or lack of authenticity. [136] "And the great dragon cast out, that old serpent, called the Devil, and Satan, which deceiveth the entire world: he was cast out into the earth, and his angels were cast out with him." Unfortunately, McConkie's comments were accepted as the truth by the members of that time.

Upon the new revelation of the church in 1978 all leaders of the church moved in a different direction concerning race. Then President Spencer W. Kimball announce to the world that the ban against blacks holding the priesthood had been lifted and the priesthood was available to all worthy men. The same Bruce McConkie stated in 1978: [137] "It does not make a particle of difference what anybody ever said about the Negro matter before the first day of June of this year, 1978. It is a new day and a new arrangement, and the Lord has now given the revelation that sheds light out into the world on this subject. As to any slivers of light or any particles of darkness of the past, we forget about them." McConkie stated forget what he or any other church leader stated before that date. McConkie invalidated all comments, Brigham Young, Joseph Feilding Smith, Himself,

---

[135] Mormon Doctrine, p. 527, 1966 ed.
[136] Revelations 12:9 (KJV)
[137] All are Alike Unto God, August 18, 1978

and others who made comments about black and dark skin that was published or not. Henceforth, one may ask how people should in or outside of the church perceive the new stand of equality compared to the previous 130 plus years of practice of inequality.

The author was initially extremely critical of the church statements and comments about dark and black skin of the past and judged the church for being racist, hypocritical, and prideful. However, over time after the disappointment, irritation, and emotions began to wane off the author developed a unique perspective with the assistance of his wife. Most people do not make righteous changes until they hit rock bottom or have a major crisis. Why should a church be any different because a church is made up of people? The church was able to lose millions of dollars if they lost their tax-exempt status for not complying with government demands about the policy of blacks in the priesthood. Then they had a revelation to change policy. It is easy to accuse the church of having a revelation over money. One must ask the question how individual people quit smoking after they learned they had lung cancer or how individual people quit drinking after they learned they had sclerosis of the liver? Worse yet, what happened to the people who did not quit smoking or drinking after a negative diagnosis? Biblically speaking, think about Saul before he became Paul on the road to Damascus in the Book of Acts. Saul was persecuting and having new Christians jailed or killed yet the Lord used him in a mighty way as he wrote half of the New Testament. The Lord changed Paul's name from Saul, changed Jacob's name to Israel, added to Abram's name as he become known as Abraham, and now the Church of Jesus Christ of Latter-Day Saints no longer refer to themselves as Mormon as of 2018. Many members of the Church of Jesus Christ of Latter-Day Saints may still identify as Mormon out of habit from the past, but the forward movement is to refer to self as a Latter Day Saint. The term Mormon refers to the prior self and is not reflective of its new direction of equality. There are claims that the church tried to distance itself from the term Mormon as early as 1982. However, the author must submit a confession.

The author was a person who began to dismiss the entire Church of Jesus Christ of Latter-Day Saints due to its past practices and beliefs and considered the church false. Select stories and statements by the church were unacceptable and unforgivable until the personal revelation of the author's own faults, flaws, and sins. The author decided to forgive Brigham Young because President Young was on the author's unfavorable list for years along with other so-called Mormon leadership. Upon, the author forgiving Brigham Young and others he felt a new freedom from the burden of holding a grudge and began to re-examine the church and The Book of Mormon. The author felt inspired to read The Book of Mormon again but this time from a historical perspective and things began to jump out to the author's understanding. It was not the book that made the early church leaders be polygamous and racist but the precepts of men. After Joseph Smith died and Brigham Young led the early saints to Utah his power and authority was unmatched and unchallenged. He was the prophet and president of the church, but he did have counselors, so the leadership was not a complete autocracy. Insomuch, if Brigham Young said he had a revelation no one was going to doubt it even though he was still a man. Henceforth, the author discovered that The Book of Mormon was not the issue but the interpretation of men.

The author believes that it is extremely ironic that a church that has multiple documentation in their own periodicals, magazines, and newspapers depicting racism could be the source that informs the world that certain people of color are the lost and scattered tribes of Israel and Judah. The 10th Article of Faith in The Church of Latter-Day Saints stated as follows. [138] "We believe in the literal gathering of Israel and in the restoration of the Ten Tribes; that Zion (the New Jerusalem) will be built upon the American continent; that Christ will reign personally upon the earth; and, that the earth will be renewed and receive its paradisiacal glory." The church stated that they believe in a real gathering of an actual people and not a spiritual reference of Israel's ten lost tribes. The research of the authors believes that the

---

[138] Articles of Faith the Church of Jesus Christ of Latter-Day Saints

lost tribes are hidden in plain sight, but most people would refuse to acknowledge evidence because people are comfortable with what they believe to be true. Insomuch, the comfort, pride, and arrogance of people could keep them from even considering evidence in front of their face could be true. Nevertheless, if the church would view the author's research even though the articles about skin color are in a negative light it could become a growing and turning point to enhance the kingdom of God and spreading the Gospel of Jesus Christ.

Chapter 11

Carnal and Spiritual Interpretations

The bible says that God is a spirit. [139] "God is a Spirit: and they that worship him must worship him in spirit and in truth." Individual early Latter-Day Saint leaders believed that God is an exalted man. The author believes the bible that God is a spirit. When the author used the search engine for the Book of Mormon online, he was unable to find where it said the God was an exalted man. Another story believed in the LDS church was that Jesus and Satan were brothers. Church leaders have used references from the Doctrine and Covenants to support this idea however the bible does not say they are brothers and neither does the Book of Mormon. A Latter-Day Saint leader once admitted that the Doctrine and Covenants are not inspired scripture so the ideas of God being an exalted man and Jesus and Satan being brothers does not have inspired scriptural support. Therefore, the author must conclude that someone or select people made up the story about God being an exalted man though individuals believe it.

Things such as men may become little gods and have their own planet are not supported by any scripture. So-called black people being less valiant in the pre-existence is not supported by scripture. So-called black people being necessary to be the seed of Cain so the devil can have representation upon the earth is not supported

---

[139] John 4:24 (KJV)

by scripture. Select men in leadership of the church were carnal and created stories that influenced the church community. The belief that a so-called black man could wash white was another belief not just of the early church but select people in the general population in earlier times. Individual people must have believed that black skin was dirty skin that could be washed clean and white. White Supremacy Theories was dominant in the 1800s for America and Europe and select unsubstantiated beliefs still linger today with individuals. The carnal nature of men is easy to address because it does not have scriptural support for its claims. However, spiritual interpretation is a different matter.

Spiritual interpretation is more challenging to deal with because two people can read the same scripture but get different ideas of its meaning. For instance, in the bible, we know that Jesus turned water into wine. Individual people interpret wine as an alcoholic beverage while other individuals say that it was grape juice without alcoholic content. The bible has examples of different interpretations of men. [140] "For one believeth that he may eat all things: another, who is weak, eateth herbs." The scriptures allow men to see things differently and not be wrong. The Gospel's of Matthew, Mark, Luke, and John tell of similar accounts of Jesus from different perspectives. However, the bible does not allow for men to change the meaning of scripture to fit one's lifestyle or make a wrong right.

Jesus would sometimes allow men to stay in their carnality. In the Book of Matthew Chapter 26 Jesus allows his audience to think carnally when he was speaking spiritually. [141] "And said, this fellow said, I can destroy the temple of God, and to build it in three days. Jesus was talking about his body resurrected in three days." Another example came with Nicodemus when He was speaking about being born again. [142] "Nicodemus saith unto him, how can a man be born when he is old? can he enter the second time into his mother's womb, and be born?" Nicodemus was thinking about a physical (carnal)

---

[140] Romans 14:2 (KJV)
[141] Matthew 26:61 (KJV)
[142] John 3:4 (KJV)

rebirth without understanding Jesus talking about a spiritual renewal. Therefore, in The Book of Mormon 2 Nephi 5:21 the early saints must have interpreted this verse in the physical (carnal). The verse states that the people received a skin of blackness because of their disobedience and sin. Therefore, anyone who has so called black skin was either sinful or their parents were sinful.

The bible says that all men have sinned. [143] "For all have sinned and come short of the glory of God." If all men have sinned should not all men have skins of blackness. Spiritually speaking we all receive a spirit skin of blackness where the light of God is not shining through us. The more people sin the more darkness comes about. Likewise, the more we try to do right and serve God the greater the light shines through us regardless of our outer complexion.

The author is not saying that all the early members of the church were carnal all the time. The fact they were trying to serve Jesus Christ as their Lord and Savior lets you know that they had spiritual awareness. They appeared spiritually hungry to learn the Word of God from the scriptures and to serve Him with maximum effort. However, they were human and a product of their environment and period in history. The bible tells us to repent and change our ways. The author believes that The Church of Jesus Christ of Latter-Day Saints is in the process of repenting. They are moving away from practices that are not scripturally supported. Just as no person is without flaw or sin neither is the church. The work of the church serving the savior is perfect work, but all individuals of every church are on different spiritual progressions. The Church of Jesus Christ of Latter- Day Saints is still predominantly composed of so-called white members but does have racial and ethnical diversity in membership and now showing more diversity in leadership and representation in the choirs and church membership. Furthermore, as a newer church formed in 1830, they had to go through growing pains, and it is difficult to digest spiritual meat when you are a spiritual babe.

The early presidents and prophets of the church especially Joseph

---

[143] Romans 3:23 (KJV)

Smith and Brigham Young held the position of Church President and Prophet at young ages still capable of producing children. The younger a person is the more they have the tendency to learn towards their carnal understandings. The author believes that both Smith and Young allowed lust to influence their revelation about polygamy which is carnal. The author heard it said that the more wives a man had the greater his status valued which is also carnal. The young church had young men teaching the word making major decisions and meaty issues. [144] "For when the time ye ought to be teachers, ye have need that one teaches you again which be the first principles of the oracles of God; and become such as have need of milk, and not of strong meat." Souls won by teaching the word beginning with issues considered milk. However, souls can choke when trying to eat meat before the spiritual maturity has manifested into its potential.

For the last one hundred years the Presidents and Prophets of The Church of Jesus Christ of Latter-Day Saints have been near 70 years of age or older and are usually grandparents or great grandparents before appointment and promotion to the highest office in the church. The men are financially stable, carnally controlled, and spiritually mature in the word and able to manage the meatier issues about the church. Their personal lust has never been a question as it was with the first two presidents. That is not to belittle the tremendous positive contributions that Joseph Smith and Brigham Young brought to the church but state that their acquisition of wives and youthful ages of individual wives are questionable by today's standards. Joseph Smith only publicly acknowledged Emma Smith as his wife during his lifetime. The latter and current leaders of the church rely heavily on each other and the different quorums when making decisions along with prayer. All meat of the spirit decisions by the church trickle down from the president and his counselors to the church which members never question or oppose. The members are confident that the leaders of the church strive hard to live right and follow the will of the Lord. The earlier members were confident

---

[144] Hebrews 5:12 (KJV)

in the leaders as well, however, may have placed them on a pedestal based upon their title and being a respecter of persons. The author spoke about select questionable comments by Brigham Young and other church leaders which the author believes individual carnal statements and decisions were made. The author had to learn that the Lord forgives us the way that we forgive others. There are still members that hold to the old Mormon ways of doing business and believing certain things not supported by the bible. Nevertheless, the church has improved regarding living closer to the Word of God but like any other denomination there will be differences between men and their perspectives.

It is comfortable for people not to change and keep their own perspectives. When a person has lived and believed in a certain way for multiple years or all their life, they think they are right in their ways and thinking. When someone comes around with a unique perspective the first tendency of most people is to reject what is different. The author is prepared for people and the Church of Jesus Christ to overlook or reject his theory about so-called black people being a large part of the lost and scattered tribes of Israel and Judah. The author is also prepared for people and the Church of Jesus Christ of Latter-Day Saints to overlook or reject that the people written about in The Book of Mormon that both Nephites and Lamanites are so-called black people from the Tribe of Joseph of the 12 Tribes of Israel. However, if the Church of Jesus Christ of Latter-Day Saints would open their minds and hearts to embrace the theology of the author it could shake up the world by seeing how one denomination went from on extreme to the other regarding people of color and their connection to the Lord.

The author is realistic and knows that people are reluctant to change their ways of thinking, especially since the author was the same way. The author grew up believing that everybody in the bible was so-called white and he loved them. The author can remember rejecting the idea that anyone in the bible was so-called black and thought only the Nation of Islam or a group of radicals produced the idea of people in the bible being anything other than white. Research done by the author over the last 8 years have shown that the people in the bible are unlikely to be so-called white. True love should have no color. The question becomes can a so-called white person love the people in the bible if they are not so-called white people. The author's hope is their color should not matter. Jesus died for the sins of all people. Jesus' genealogy in the books of Matthew and Luke show that He had so-called undesirable bloodlines in his lineage. Henceforth, nobody on earth today has a pure bloodline and color should not matter.

Part Five
The Author's Theology

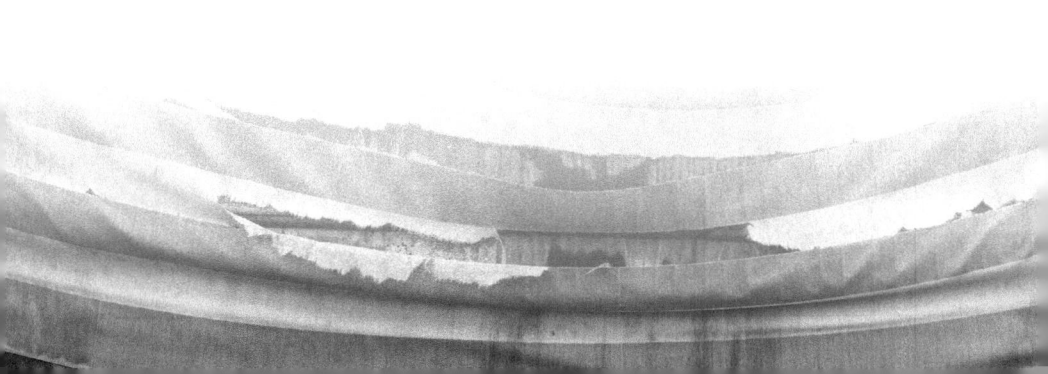

PART FIVE

THE AUTHOR'S THEOLOGY

CHAPTER 12
OVERVIEW OF THE AUTHOR'S THEOLOGY

The overview of the author's theology begins and ends with what the bible says about the Lord creating heaven and earth and how we all need a Savior which is Jesus Christ. The title of this book "America Accept the Truth, Repent, and Save Our Country: Drop the Hate and Communicate the Love of Christ" is also the mission and purpose of the author. The author believes that the least respected people on earth which are the so-called black people in the Americas are part of the lost and scattered tribes. The author focused on the Americas, but the bible said the lost and scattered tribes were dispersed to the four corners of the earth and there are so-called black people on every continent. The theology by the author was not developed until the year 2018 when he discovered according to the Zondervan Bible Dictionary that the Negro people were not descendants of Noah's son Ham. It was already established by biblical scholars and seen in the Book of Jubilees that Ham's descendants went to the south, which is known as Africa today, Japheth's descendants went to the north, which is known as Europe, which left the Negros to be descendants of Shem which is the family line discussed throughout the bible leading up to Jesus Christ. Henceforth, the author believes that so-called black people suffer more than other races not because of inferiority but due to turning their back on God and choosing Barabbas over Jesus lost their protection from strangers and enemies. Henceforth, so called blacks in general are still choosing Barabbas over Jesus because modern day Barabbas represents danger, excitement, with street credibility while modern day Jesus is considered peaceful, dull, with too many restrictions.

If so-called black people repent and turn their heart back to God and accept Jesus Christ as their Lord and Savior, they can reverse the curse they have been under according to Deuteronomy Chapter 28. Insomuch, the following paragraphs and pages in the chapter "Overview of the Author's Theology" will be supporting and providing background to the author's perspective.

The author believes that Jesus Christ walked this earth without sin and became the perfect sacrifice for humankind. Jesus later crucified, bled, and died for the sins of all men in which He was placed in a tomb and rose again three days later claiming the keys to life, death, and hell becoming the bridge to God and Heaven. The author believes that we saved by grace, not of works, and eternal life is about accepting Jesus Christ as our personal Lord and Savior, and He is the only way to God and Heaven. [145] "For it is written, As I live, saith the Lord, every knee shall bow to me, and every tongue shall confess to God." The author loves this verse because regardless of what a person's belief, religion, or view of life they are going to one day recognize Jesus as Lord regardless of their faith or lack of. Unfortunately, individual people either do not read the scriptures, do not accept the gospel of Jesus Christ, or may be fully turned against Jesus or any type of religion.

Different religions and various denominations are part of a complicated scheme to divide men against each other. Within denominations we have division and within the same denomination you can find conflict between individuals. Jesus once accused of casting out demons in the adversary's name and He spoke about how the same kingdom cannot be divided against itself and maintain its strength. [146] "And if Satan revolt against himself, and be divided, he

---

[145] Romans 14:11 (KJV)
[146] Matthew 12:26 (KJV)

cannot stand, but hath an end." Insomuch, God cannot be divided against God and stand either. That is why the Father (God), Jesus Christ (Son), and The Holy Spirit/Ghost are perfectly unified as one. Trying to understand the ways of God can be mind boggling to the human brain. People have the tendency to disrespect what they do not understand and dismiss it. People can also be prideful and arrogant, wanting to act like they know and understand everything even when they do not know or understand something. The bible said that God would reveal things to babes instead of revealing to a prideful or arrogant person. However, sometimes God gives us revelations to where He allows us to understand a certain aspect that He wants revealed to us.

The author understands that his view about the lost and scattered tribes of Israel and Judah may receive rejection by certain groups. The author believes that the group of people that best fit the curses of Deuteronomy 28 are the so-called African American people in the United States. Darker skinned people across the planet are often considered the lowest groups of people regarding prosperity and civilization. If the author is correct, it by no means elevates so called African Americans to a higher level above other people regarding their covenant with The Most- High God. However, the covenant with God does let us know that they are not below any people. No other people on the planet were stripped of their name, their religion, and knowledge of their history the way that so-called African Americans have in this country. Even the Jews who suffered through the Holocaust still knew their name, their religion, and their history. Insomuch, lets address the current state of the Jewish nation.

The author will not call who we know as Jews fake Jews. A person can be a Jew by converting or being born to parents in the religion of Judaism. A person can be an Israelite by relocating to Israel or being born in Israel. The largest sect of Jews today is the Ashkenazi Jews, and the second largest sect are the Sephardic Jews. A person is identified as Jewish today through matrilineal ancestry. The author found it interesting that the bible identifies bloodlines through patrilineal ancestry. However, the author believes that the modern patrilineal ancestry records were lost through war, captivity, slavery, integration, intermingling, and sexual violence but the matrilineal records were well preserved. Therefore, it was wise that the children of Ashkenaz (Japheth) kept records of their Jewish (Shem) connections through the mother's bloodline. There are Ashkenazi Jews in the United States prospering in various industries such as business, law, medical, entertainment, banking, and other fields. Henceforth, one could rationalize that the people the world recognizes as Jews today possibly reap the benefits of obeying the Laws of God in Deuteronomy 28 such as to lend and not borrow.

In the Book of Genesis when Noah awoke from his drunken episode, he set blessings and cursing's. [147] "And he said, Blessed be the LORD God of Shem; and Canaan shall be his servant." In the King James Version Noah blessed the God of Shem he did not bless Shem. Therefore, if Shem obeys and blesses God, he is blessed but if the people of Shem do not obey and bless God, they could lose their favor. Canaan and being a servant is a different topic. The next verse in Genesis Chapter 9 Noah makes a pronouncement over Japheth. [148] "God shall enlarge Japheth, and he shall dwell in the tents of Shem; and Canaan shall be his servant." Noah did not call Japheth's enlargement a blessing but said that they would be enlarged, and God would allow it. Noah also said that Japheth would dwell in the tents of Shem. He did not say that it would be because of mutual agreement. It is possible that Japheth overtook the tents of Shem either by force or abandonment. Insomuch, one might consider that Japheth replaced Shem in the tents and Noah prophesied that Shem would not be in its former tents if they did not honor God of Shem which Christians and Jews refer to as the God of Abraham, Isaac, and Jacob.

One of the blessings of Deuteronomy 28:12 is that God would bless and reward his people that they would lend to nations and not borrow. We know today that the most powerful banks are owned by

---

[147] Genesis 9:26 (KJV)
[148] Genesis 9:27 (KJV)

what we know as Jewish people. Stating the facts of who owns are controls a business is not antisemitic just as stating that most professional basketball are black is not a racist statement. Is it possible that Jews who adopted Judaism or Matrilineal Jews were more obedient to the commandments and principalities of God than the Patrilineal Jews and became blessed and cursed accordingly? In the bible the Israelites and Jews went through periods of blessings through obedience, slavery, and oppression when they were disobedient to Gods word. Their slavery and oppression could last through generations of people and hundreds of years. The bible shows there is a commitment to the covenant of the blood line people, but faith is more important than bloodline. The bible does warn us about Jews who are not Jews in Revelations 2:9 and 3:9 and says they are the synagogue of Satan. However, the author will not contradict the bible, nor will he assume that every person of European descent who calls themselves a Jew is of the synagogue of Satan.

The author believes that a small percentage of people, much lower than one percent of the world are so-called running/controlling the world. These people whoever they may be are in positions of high places and that it is why it is important for the Body of Christ to be aware and always protected. [149] "For we wrestle not against flesh and blood, but against principalities, against powers, against the rulers of the darkness of this world, against spiritual wickedness in high places." Upon Christ return to earth as mentioned in the Book of Revelation His authority will trump all but until then Satan has his people in place hidden in plain sight. There are rumors of elite families that most do not know enough about to discuss in detail. The author does know that the serpent has a seed according to Genesis 3:15 where the woman's seed will bruise the serpent seeds head and serpent seed will bruise the woman's seed heels. The biting of heals may represent that he makes it hard to stand up or walk in righteousness making each step painful. However, through Christ

---

[149] Ephesians 6:12 (KJV)

the main head crusher of Satan He will triumph over all of Satan's plans.

The famous bible verse John 3:16 stated: [150] "For God so loved the world, that he gave his only begotten Son, that whosoever believeth in him should not perish, but have everlasting life." The key part is whosoever believeth in him should not perish but have everlasting life. We must believe in Jesus Christ as our savior given to us by God. The bible does not say only a certain race can have everlasting life. The author believes that God is not concerned with our skin color, nationality, ethnicity, socioeconomic status, educational background, or any other thing the world places value on. One must ask the question, why does man place so much emphasis on worldly things? Henceforth, what influences man to think the way he does?

The media influence over the thought process of mankind cannot be ignored. The media of the airway's television, radio, cell phones, and the internet can distribute information in seconds to millions and billions of people. Print media such as newspapers, books, magazines, posters, flyers, and so forth can have a strong effect on people but it does not reach the masses as quickly as the airways. The bible refers to Satan as being the prince of the power of the air. [151] "Wherein in time past ye walked according to the course of this world, according to the prince of the power of the air, the spirit that now worketh in the children of disobedience." The media are manipulated by those who are in authority over the media to garner sympathy or invoke anger to whatever their objective may be. The media will often seek sympathy for poor Jews in Russia and Ukraine to garner public financial support for them. Unfortunately, what nobody is talking about is what the bible says about the lost and scattered Jews and Israel is that they will not know who they are and hidden from themselves.

The Ashkenazi Jews and Sephardic Jews know who they are and have European descent. Again, the author accepts that modern Jews are from the maternal lineage. Pastors John and Matthew Hagee are

---

[150] John 3:16 (KJV)
[151] Ephesians 2:2 (KJV)

the biggest supporters of Israel in America. John Hagee has testified how he became blessed since he began supporting Israel and he will never stop. Giving and supporting people in need is a biblical principle that God will bless those who bless others. The intent of our hearts is more important to God than if the person/group is honest or deceiving regarding an issue or situation. People who are deceiving or receiving in fraud are judged accordingly. Therefore, a person should continue giving or doing in any area that they believe find favor with God.

The author has a slight fear and warning for the American people. What if the paternal birthright lineage of the Jews and Israelites are right in your backyard in the form of so-called African Americans and Native Americans? What is your personal record of how you treat, support, or help so-called African Americans and Native Americans? Did you ignore injustice, call injustice righteousness, or think that individual people get what they deserve? Jesus said his first conceived mission was not for all people. [152] "But he answered and said, I am not sent but unto the lost sheep of the house of Israel." Jesus did lay down His life for all who would accept Him, but He sought to reclaim the lost sheep of Israel. One thing should be clear whether a person is a Jew, Gentile, Protestant, Catholic, or whatever the religion may be if Christ is not accepted as Lord and Savior, you do not have the promise of eternal life with God. The people we know as Jews today do not believe that Jesus was the Messiah. There have been individual Jews that have converted to Christianity, but the Jews are waiting for a different Messiah. Yet, America sends billions of dollars to Israel in financial aid each year. One must ask if the financial support to Israel political or spiritual. Henceforth, the author suggests even though America's foundation was supposed to be Christian based the financial aid seems to be more political than spiritual.

There are select reasons the author believes the financial support to Israel is political. Israel has oil, and its location is near other top

---

[152] Matthew 15:24 (KJV)

oil producing nations in the Middle East. Israel has nuclear weapons which seems odd for a country that reformed in 1948. It would appear the military support from the United States protects Israel from major attacks even though the region can be volatile at times. Lastly, the author believes that the bible speaks about the paternal Jews and Israelis as the lost and scattered tribes and not the maternal lineage based upon the bible's genealogical records.

The author has good experiences with people who are known as Jews today. Hate crimes against Jews or any other group of people is not acceptable. The author belief that modern day Israelis and Jews not being the same as biblical Jews actual comes from brave Jews who admitted that they are not the same Jews. The Jews who came forward with information about Jews let the author know that all modern-day Jews are not from the synagogue of Satan as mentioned in Revelations 2:9 and 3:9. Ironically, the organization known as the Ku Klux Klan has been quoted as hating Jews (modern day) and Negroes (so-called black people). Henceforth, the Klan hates both the maternal and (paternal Jews) who only know themselves as negro/colored/black/African American.

Hate in any form is evil and not from God. Ironically, the Ku Klux Klan has members that claim to be Christian and do the work of the Lord by causing terror in individuals and groups they hate. In the New Testament we learn to love the Lord thy God with all thy heart, mind, and strength. We are instructed to love our neighbor as ourselves. All people are our neighbors. Even though all people should be our neighbors most people have favorite and least favorite neighbors. The bible has examples of favoritism within their families such as Jacob and his son Joseph whom he gave the coat of colors. The bible also spoke of how Isaac favored Esau and Rebecca favored Jacob. The bible never said it was right to have favoritism, but it did not directly say it was wrong either. Favoritism of people is almost inevitable because people will look after their household and family first. Prejudice is common and sometimes happens without people thinking based upon the environment a person was raised in. Prejudice can be corrected by people who are willing to look at themselves. Racism is an evil act of intentionally oppressing, discriminating, degrading, or mistreating an individual or group based upon bias differences of race. Individual people of all races may display prejudice but very few people are racist because a racist is a person of influence and power who can negatively affect a person's life and way of living. People who experience prejudice may feel anger, sadness, resentment, or aspects of bullying. Prejudice behavior is usually an impulse or reaction, but racism is usually calculated and planned. Henceforth, the author believes hiding the identity of the lost and scattered tribes of Israel and Judah was planned and calculated.

There are a group of people who say they are the term woke or awake to the truths of a people that have been hidden. A group called the Hebrew Israelites in America is a group of men and women of color who believe they are descendants of the scattered tribes of Israel in the bible. Biologically in the flesh they may be right however if they don't have Jesus/Yeshua they are missing salvation. The author is not an expert on the Hebrew Israelites but has learned there are different sects and camps to the group in which individuals range from peaceful to extreme. The author witnessed select videos of Hebrew Israelites teaching in the streets of select cities while individuals were teaching from the bible and made select believable points. However, select messages overshadowed by negative activity of screaming or berating so-called white people and so-called black Christian clergy to prove their point.

It has become clear to the author that information and knowledge without discernment of the spirit is dangerous. We need guidance by the Holy Spirit to guide our actions and the way that we treat people. It does not do any good for our salvation if we can prove that we are of the bloodline of Abraham, Isaac, and Jacob but we do not accept Jesus Christ as our Lord and Savior. The author went through a period of seeking knowledge but did not always use a discerning spirit which caused different emotions to arise. The author went through a period of transition and anger from being deceived. The author found out the origin of the letter J. The author found out that the letter J founded around the year 1524 according to a Google search after learning about it from a video. That means that Jesus was called by a different name while He was on the earth. His Hebrew name is Yeshua along with other spellings and pronunciations. The author learned about the Catholic Church appointing December 25th as Jesus birthday and appointing the Holiday of Easter. It was also the Catholic Church that made Sunday be the Sabbath Day and gave the world the term Trinity. During this time and before the author was discovering the racism in the Mormon church which contributed to ill feelings towards groups of people. The author no longer has any bitterness towards any people, groups, or religions. Acquiring information and gaining knowledge gives a person a feeling of superiority because they know something another person does not know. After the author's quest for knowledge and information began to stagnate, he learned that what really matters is the relationship between a person and God and if they accepted Jesus/Yeshua or whatever name in their language they give to the Messiah. The author is not saying that knowledge and information is not important but that it is less important than the relationship with God through Jesus Christ and doing and living the Lord's will for our lives. Unfortunately, there are so many people who do not have a relationship with the Lord and do not know they have special ties to the people in the bible.

To identify the lost and scattered tribes of Israel and Judah the author simply looked at the most lost and scattered people on the planet today. The people with the least sense of identity, esteem, and knowledge about their history was unquestionable the so-called black people on the planet. So-called African Americans are the only people on the planet identified by two continents. There is also an issue that Americans who are descendants from Europe are referred as American instead of European American where people who were already here are called Native Americans. We have Asian Americans who know if they are Japanese, Chinese, Korean, Filipino, Vietnamese, or any other Asian country. We have Hispanic Americans who know if they are Mexican, Puerto Rican,

Cuban, or any other Spanish speaking country. People in America who descended from Europe know if they have bloodlines to the English, German, French, Polish, or any other European nation. Native Americans can tell you what tribe they are from such as Seminole, Apache, Comanche, Hopi, or any other tribes. Africans who live in Africa can tell you if they are Kenyan, Sudanese, South African, Nigerian, Egyptian, Ghana, or any other African nation. However, the African American cannot tell you where they are from because their history, language, and religion stripped away from them leaving them without a true sense of identity.

The discovery of the 1747 English map of Negroland in a message from Pastor Stephen Darby and learning from the Zondervan Bible Dictionary that the Negro was not a descendant of Ham the son of Noah in the bible inspired additional research. Since all human beings either descended from Ham, Shem, or Japheth and Negros were not from Ham that meant they were either from Shem or Japheth. Biblical Scholars have long stated that Europeans came from Japheth and had lighter skin tones. Therefore, Negros had to come from the line of Shem. The revelation helped clarify in the authors mind how in the Book of Genesis how Joseph of the twelve tribes of Israel was not recognized by his brothers who thought he was Egyptian because they had similar skin tone. It also explained how Moses was able to pass as Egyptian and raised by Pharaoh's daughter because of similar skin tones. Furthermore, it explained how Joseph and Mary were able to hide baby Jesus from Herod in Egypt because of similar skin tones.

Further research done by the author after learning about a historian named Dane Calloway who claimed that so-called Negros were here long before Columbus so-called discovered America and were the true Native Americans. Mr. Calloway's research conflicted with the author's prior knowledge of the Atlantic Slave trade. Upon researching the author discovered that over 90% of the Native Americans died either through genocide or diseases they received from the Europeans on American soil. Furthermore, individual Columbus men raped, prostituted, beat, and killed select native women and men. The discovery about Columbus was disappointing and disgusting to the author and it exposed how information was manipulated to serve an agenda. Lastly, when the author revisited The Book of Mormon and read that the family that sailed to the Americas around 600 B.C. were descendants of Joseph from the 12 Tribes of Israel made things began to come together for the author. Insomuch, the timeline of 600 B.C. coincided with a Biblical Historical Timeline stating that Native Americans/Indians roots were discovered in the Americas around 600 B.C.

One could argue that the author's theology is based upon assumptions and coincidences. However, are not all theories based upon assumptions and coincidences of available information. The Atlantic Slave Trade brought Negros to the United States, Caribbean, and South America.[153] "The 1747 Map of Africa which included a place called Negroland would provide Negros with a land of origin." Upon further research the people who migrated to Negroland were people who escaped persecution and slavery of the Romans in Jerusalem starting in 70 AD. That would mean the people in Negroland were not Hamitic/African but Semitic from either the tribes if Israel or Judah. One of the missions of slave capturers and slave owners in America was to wipe away the language of the slaves, give the slaves English names, wipe away their religion, and inject what they wanted their slaves to believe. Eventually, out of fear and conditioning the slaves would forget their origins over generations and indoctrinated into a subservient sense of self.

Over time to keep slaves from gaining knowledge the owners made it illegal for slaves to learn how to read, the 1747 Map of Africa disappeared, mental, physical, and emotional abuse/indoctrination was in effect. A major part of the indoctrination of slaves came from what is known as the Willie Lynch Theory. This was a letter or series of letters (per Judge Joe Brown) that taught slave owners how to control their slaves and they would remain self-managed for generations to come. The author will not go into the details about the

---

[153] Map of Negroland https://www.loc.gov/item/2018585377/

Willie Lynch Letter that individual people claim is a myth. However, upon the author reading the so-called mythical letter from a Google search and later order a copy of the text he could see evidence that the intended result of the letter is still working and self-managing people who would consider descendants of former slaves' people today. The major design of the Willie Lynch Letter was to turn the enslaved people against each other by age, gender, status (house and field workers), and skin tone (individual slave masters intentionally impregnated female slaves) to cause division. The lighter skinned slaves favored by the masters and resented by the darker skinned slaves. Today so-called African Americans are the most divided people on the planet. From Marcus Garvey & W.E.B. DuBois to Martin Luther King & Malcom X (initially), and to conservatives (rich or professional class) and liberals (working class or poor) the house and field negro mentality still exist. Ironically, over time the term Negro disappeared as the terms for this group of people went from Negro, to Colored, to Mulatto if mixed races, to Black, and currently African American.

The term African American suggest that all people of color/black are from Africa. The term Negro vilified by the derogatory nickname associated with it to the point the group of people would resist reclaiming being called a Negro. Therefore, a person who is from Africa or a person who does not acknowledge being a Negro cannot claim to be from the Lost and Scattered Tribes of Israel and Judah. Black Hebrew Israelites who claim to be from the Lost and Scattered Tribes of Israel and Judah and have made the claim long before the author authored this book. It should be noted that not all Hebrew Israelites are radicals who scream and berate people. To the author's understanding individual Hebrew Israelites are God loving people who read the scriptures and share what they have learned. The author has never attended a meeting or had a conversation with a person claiming to be a Hebrew Israelite but deemed it necessary to include the Hebrew Israelites in this book because they claim to be the bloodline of the biblical Hebrews which is the basis of the author identifying the lost and scattered tribes. Nevertheless, the author is a follower of Christ and what the Savior emphasizes important for us to do in this earthly realm and spreading his gospel and that is the focus of the author.

In summary the author believes the New Testament instructs believers to spread the gospel of Jesus Christ to all nations. The Apostle Paul preached the gospel to the gentiles, and gentiles have been doing an excellent job spreading the gospel across the globe. The author believes that gentiles are of European descent. The author believes it's shameful that it is lost in many history books the kindness and support of so-called white Americans who were against slavery and helped negros to freedom. Also lost is how many so-called white Americans were positive supporters of the Civil Rights movement. Individual Christian missionaries of various denominations, ethnicities, and race have been busy taking the gospel to various parts of the world. The bible translated into individual languages and distributed to people, so they could read the bible in their native tongue. Television stations created with a Christian format reaching people who need the gospel and who are home bound and unable to go to church. Evangelist have been seeking people a various backgrounds, races, ethnicities, and other differences letting people know that the gospel belongs to everyone who will accept it. The bible is clear about those who accept Jesus Christ as their Lord and Savior and live accordingly to the best of their ability saved and those who reject Christ denied before God into the Kingdom of Heaven.

According to the bible there will be a judgment of people including America. God chastises those He loves, and He loves everyone. God also has a covenant people in Israel and Judah. God's covenant people dishonored the covenant and they have been chastised hundreds and thousands of years for non-repentance. However, God is faithful to His covenant people and the bible says that He will restore them. God's covenant people wanted to participate in the things of the world and the ways of the gentiles and God did not interfere. However, the behavior did not have a good outcome for God's covenant people, and they ended up suffering the curses of Deuteronomy 28 including going into slavery multiple times.

The author believes that the so-called black man needs to stop blaming the so-called white man and the government for being in a position of being oppressed and mistreated. The author knows oppression and mistreatment is real in America however through observation focusing on the oppressors has not changed the outcome for the masses. Henceforth, the so-called white man and government should not be viewed as god. There is a higher power. So-called black people are not in oppressed situations because of anybody other than our ancestor's decision to disobey God and break the covenant they had with God. When so-called black people were honoring the covenant with God they were protected from their enemies. However, when so-called black people desired to be like other nations including the gentiles, they became disobedient, dishonored the covenant, and lost its hedge of protection of the Almighty God. God teaches lessons to those He loves, and so-called black people have been taught a lesson, but God is faithful, and He will redeem His covenant people. God is waiting for His covenant people to repent and when they do so they can reverse the curse. Individually, so-called black people can prosper. Individuals are prospering by choosing God and individuals have prospered by choosing the way of the world and are exploited for their talents and ability to entertain and make money. Nevertheless, God never said that it was acceptable to intentionally mistreat His covenant people and those who did will be judged.

The author advises people who intentionally mistreat other people to repent. People who seem beneath you may be God's covenant people that an individual would be accountable for. This is beyond a race or ethnicity thing because all people regardless of complexion have people of different races somewhere in their genealogy. The author believes that people should stop the foolishness, love our neighbors as ourselves just as the bible instructs us. The reason the author believes that it is important to identify the lost and scattered tribes of Israel and Judah is because individual people are lost in their identity and have been taught, they are second class citizens, and that God does not love them the same. If people knew that God loved them, they would learn to trust Him and believe in Him. There is nothing more impowering than knowing that you do not have to spend your mortal life feeling guilty, unworthy, and unloved. The world would be better if all people accepted Jesus Christ as their Lord and Savior. Unfortunately, the bible tells us that everyone will not accept Jesus Christ as Lord and Savior. Therefore, servants of the Lord should try to reach as many people as possible to encourage people to accept the truth, repent, and save our country by dropping all forms of hate and communicate the grace of Our Lord and Savior Jesus Christ.

Part Six
Backlash

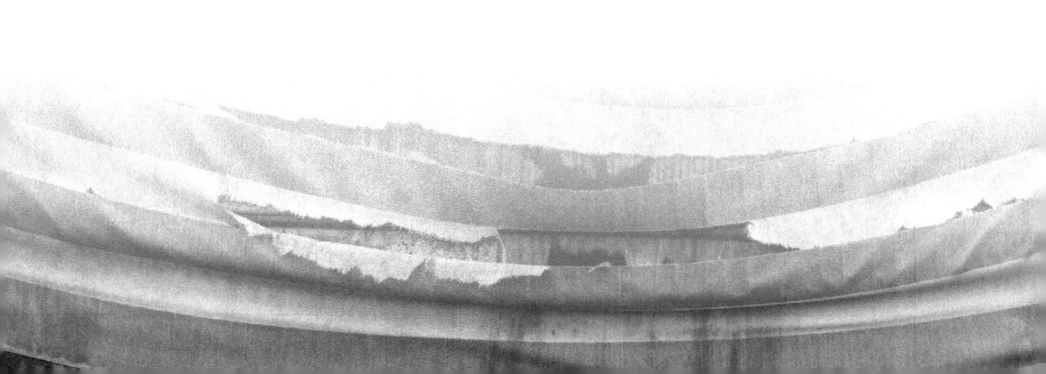

Chapter 13

Backlash From Bible Traditionalist

The bible traditionalist has been conditioned to the social norms of society of who is who as portrayed by the media and what individuals were taught growing up. Bible traditionalist are good people who believe in God and accept Jesus Christ as their Lord and Savior. Bible traditionalists try to show good will towards all men and try to live a life that is pleasing to God. Traditionalists are not people who easily accept change or different thought processes. Traditionalists are comfortable with believing the way their parents believed and doing things the way the people before them did things. Therefore, how things are perceived regarding the bible, race, ethnicity, gender, sexuality, socioeconomic background, education, and so forth meaning how things are and are how things are always meant to be.

    To gain a better perspective on how traditionalists formulated their thoughts and opinions about the bible and religion the author had to delve into the past and the most influential aspects of the topic. The gentiles received the Gospel of Jesus Christ from the Apostle Paul who was a Benjamite of the 12 Tribes of Israel. The gentiles appeared to receive and accept the Gospel of Jesus Christ more willingly than the Jews did. Though individual Jews converted to Christianity individual gentiles were willing to continues spreading the gospel of Christ. The Romans were the military and political powerhouse nation at the time that Christ walked the earth and hundreds years after Jesus was crucified. Insomuch, that overtime the image of Jesus was shaped by the gentiles who had power and influence.

The painting by Leonardo Da Vinci called the "Last Supper" resonates in the minds of most people who call themselves Christian. Jesus is sitting in the middle of a table surrounded by the twelve disciples breaking bread before Judas will leave to portray Him. Images are powerful and stick in the minds of people. The painting by Michelangelo "God and Man" where a naked Adam is reaching out with his finger to touch the finger of God is also a powerful image implanted in the minds of those who have seen the artwork. The Pope of their times commissioned paintings to create the impact upon people of that time. Most people in the 15th and 16th century did not read so paintings were created to help people know the stories in the bible. Henceforth, as the author fast forwards to the American culture there is another aspect of shaping images and thoughts more powerful than paintings.

Drawings and paintings continue to shape the images in people to this day but in the 20th century the powerful medium of movies and television was born. Think about the word television which is sampling saying that it is telling a vision. The question is whose vision, is it? During the authors journey to learn more about the bible he watched old movies such as "The 10 Commandments with Charlton Heston as Moses", "Moses" with Burt Lancaster, "The Greatest Story Ever Told", "The Bible", "Ben Hur", "David and Bathsheba", "King David", "The Passion of Christ", and other movies and television shows. There was a great push in Hollywood to create biblical movies in the 1950s and early 1960s to promote their version of the bible in an entertaining way. Movies and shows were created beyond those decades even until today. All the lead characters from the bible were played by so-called white actors and actresses. Occasionally, the movie would show a so-called black person or people in the background with non-speaking roles depicting an Egyptian or Ethiopian in a servant role. The actor Sidney Portier was in a biblical movie once as the so-called black man who helped Jesus carry His cross. Regardless, of a person's race or ethnicity when you watch movies or see images of biblical figures portrayed as having white skin you believe the images you have seen are truthful.

Traditionalists may have a tough time letting go of their traditional beliefs, but they also believe in the truth. Individual traditionalists may be able to accept something different from what they have always believed to be true, but the distinct perspective will have to be presented in a convincing way with solid support and facts. They author's goal with traditionalist consists of opening their eyes to the possibility that his research is valid but more importantly to treat all people with respect regardless of a person's race or ethnicity because they will fulfill God's New Testament commandment to "Love thy Neighbor as Thyself." Therefore, if people treat each other with kindness, respect, and hospitality that will portray individuals as ambassadors of Christ and guide more people to The Gospel of Jesus Christ.

Chapter 14

Backlash From White Supremacist

All so-called white people are not White Supremacist nevertheless those who are White Supremacist may have a backlash to the author's perspective. White Supremacist think everything white is right and everything and everybody else is wrong and beneath them. Individual White Supremacists believe that so-called black people are ignorant, lazy, and animalistic such as monkey and ape like. Not all White Supremacists think alike and have various levels of education but seem to have a common interest to control or instill fear in those they deem beneath them. All White Supremacist are not part of hate groups. Hate groups seem to think all things white are right but as a group they do not have political influence, business ownership, or superior finances to affect the living conditions of other classifications of people. However, there are individuals within hate groups that may have the political influence, business ownership, and superior finances to affect other groups of people.

Hate groups must be discussed briefly because everything they believe has been taught to them. Babies and children are not born to hate or mistreat people because of their race. Individual adult or older children pass the theology of supremacy to the youth, and it is unfortunate. People have the right to feel however they feel but they do not have the right to cause pain and discomfort to people because they do not like them. Henceforth, the author will discuss select hate crimes that have taken place in the United States.

Hate crimes in the United States has touched everyone. In 2021-22 there was a rise in Asian hate crimes. People of European descent are not immune either and receive the teasing and maltreatment for being Polish, Irish, and especially Jewish. On the 1970s television show "All in the Family" a character named Archie Bunker played by the actor Carroll O' Conner was portrayed as a bigot (primarily to expose bigotry in America) and he continually made racially insensitive remarks and disrespectful terms as calling his Polish son in law a Pollock. So-called Native Americans suffered disrespect for years especially in professional sports nicknames which indicates the Native Americans as savages. In the year 2021-22 The former Washington Redskins dropped the name Redskins and their logo. The former Cleveland Indians followed suit and dropped their nickname and logo to become the Cleveland Commanders. The moves to change the names and logos are a step in the right direction regarding racial and ethnic sensitivity. Negative stereotypes of Hispanics and derogatory names have been commonplace as racial and ethnical insensitivity. Hollywood is the worst offender of perpetrating stereotypes to fit the White Supremacy perspective. So-called black people were made fun of in minstrel shows where a so-called white actor would color their face black and perpetrate their producer's idea of black behavior and mannerisms as stereotypes for entertainment. The shows were impressionable upon society and created negative opinions of so-called black people as being lazy, slow talking, sex crazed, criminals, and have no ability to lead people. Hollywood stereotypes could be a chapter or a book by itself. Nevertheless, the worst treatment of people in the United States because of White Supremacy has been to the so-called Negro, Black, African American people.

Thankfully, to cell phones and video cameras the mistreatment of so-called black people has been recorded for all to judge and see. In recent times George Floyd was filmed being choked to death by an officer of the law who refused to adhere to Mr. Floyd saying that he could not breathe. A gentleman by the name of Eric Garner was also filmed being choked by an officer years earlier. There have been countless so-called black people shot and killed not only by law enforcement but by citizens who received little to no consequence for their actions. A riot was started in Los Angeles California in the 1990s when Rodney King was videotaped being beaten by police and the officers were not found guilty. People in the so-called black community can tell stories about events of murder without consequence that has taken place for decades and even centuries. The author is not focused on law enforcement in this book because he believes the good officers far outweigh the bad ones, but the purpose of the author is to show the inequality a race of people was mistreated and few to nobody spoke against the treatment of the group of people. Unfortunately, what we have learned is how little White Supremacy values the lives of so- called black people. It should be mentioned that in the George Floyd case individual people of different racial backgrounds put particularly so-called white people stepped up and spoke up against the choking death of Mr. Floyd. The Christian community in general, not including the Public Relations of Reverend Al Sharpton or Reverend Jesse Jackson who collaborate with local black churches when highly publicized incidents occur remain silent on issues of race and law enforcement. Insomuch, the author believes that Jesus would be considered a radical by today's standards and that all Christians need to stand up and be heard when things need to change to make a better world.

In the 1800 and 1900s so-called black people were hung to death on trees (lynching), burned at stakes, killed by other means, beaten, and raped at the discretion of the perpetrator without consequence. No human being should have the right to take the life or emotionally and physically damage another for being different. White Supremacy made people feel they had rights that they did not have. Nevertheless, the law was on the side of White Supremacist. In the United States the 1800s up until the mid-1960s there were "White Only" restrooms and drinking fountains in various parts of the country. Certain restaurants and hotels would not serve so-called negros, blacks, or coloreds as were the terms of those days. Athletes and entertainers in the 40s, 50s, and sixties such as Jackie Robinson, Muhammad Ali, Jim Brown, Bill Russell, and Kareem Abdul-Jabbar just to name a few so-called African Americans who stood up and spoke against the mistreatment of celebrities of color during those times. A non-white person could get arrested if they attempted to use or confront management about using a certain restroom, drinking fountain, restaurant, or hotel. The credibility of the accuser or the accuracy of the claim against a person of color was rarely considered prior to the Civil Rights Act of 1964. Justice for people of color after 1964 remains questionable as there were cases prior to DNA and video footage that were based upon speculation and circumstantial evidence. The saddest part is how Christian White Supremacist could justify the mistreatment of a group of people using a bible that says do not murder. The bible did say (paraphrasing) to Israel and Judah who were scattered that because of their disobedience and disregard to the covenant that they would lose the protection that the Lord gave them, and they were in subjection to the oppressors. However, even though the Lord temporarily lifted His protection He heard the cries of His people and those who were guilty would have to answer for their sins and mistreatment of humanity. Henceforth, please repent America.

The author wants to make it clear that he does not think most so-called white people are White Supremacist. During the times of the Trans-Atlantic Slave Trade very few people were slave owners and today very few people outwardly display hostility toward other races. Racial hostility is still alive, and it resurfaced during the Obama and Trump presidential administrations, but most people outwardly preferred peaceful interactions. Interracial couples and multiracial children are ever increasing to the point that most families today have biracial relationships or children. During the days of Dr. Martin Luther King and prior to him one of the greatest fears of White Supremacist was interracial relationships of biracial children. A boy named Emmet Till was dragged and killed in the 1950s for whistling at a so-called white woman that he found attractive. The fear is if whites and blacks continue to intermix that the so-called white race will be eliminated. By the laws at the time varied by state but the "One Drop Rule" made a person considered black or colored. Individual states would say that less than 1/eighth blood could make a person considered white and 1/fourth depending on the outward appearance of a person. [154] "In the United States, the "one-drop rule" — also known as hypodescent — dates to a 1662 Virginia law on the treatment of mixed-race individuals." [155] "The legal notion of hypodescent has been upheld as recently as 1985, when a Louisiana court ruled that a woman with a black great-great-great-great-grandmother could not identify herself as "white" on her passport." Henceforth, based upon the law that White Supremacist were part of creating, it is easy to see why they wanted to keep so-called whites and blacks separate.

The worst part of White Supremacy is not the hate crimes but the extreme measures they went to manipulate history and make everything white seem good and pure and everything black insignificant or evil. Over 99 percent of so-called white people had nothing to do with the shaping of history, but they still benefited from the positive portrayal while other races were omitted or portrayed in a negative light which created negative self-esteem issues for individuals. The effects of individuals thinking they are less than others limit their ability to prosper. Individuals who feel limited or believe that there is a glass ceiling above their ability to achieve may tend to settle where they are in their career, or only do enough to get by. Individual people tend to give up on life on this earth because things seem stacked against them which creates feelings of hopelessness. People who feel hopeless are usually easier to control or manipulate through fear and intimidation. White Supremacist want to keep so-called black people in their place. Individuals who do not fear and stand against the norm of White Supremacy used to end up beaten, incarcerated, or killed as an example for others not to oppose

---

[154] Bradt, Steve. https://news.harvard.edu/gazette/story/2010/12/one-drop-rule-persists/

[155] Bradt, S. https://news.harvard.edu/gazette/story/2010/12/one-drop-rule-persists/

their system. However, individuals overcome perceived limitations and prosper and have good success. but that is not the majority.

The bottom line is any feelings of supremacy are wrong whether it is white, black, or indifferent. The purpose of the author speaking of this topic is to bring awareness and for those who may fit the category of being a White Supremacist to repent and change their ways. It may take an act of God the way it took for Saul who became Paul to change in the bible, but the possibility is there.

The author anticipates backlash from White Supremacist more than any other group because his research completely contradicts the ways and thinking of so-called White Supremacist. Insomuch, the author anticipates hatred from people who really do not know or understand his perspective because his perspective is in direct opposition to the views of White Supremacy. That is not to say the author agrees with Black Supremacy because he does not but, the author is for the equality of all people and reviewing the facts and considering different interpretations of the information. Prayerfully, any backlash would be minor and not to the magnitude of hate crimes of the past. Matthew 22:39 says to love thy neighbor as thyself which can be difficult when you believe that someone hates you. Nevertheless, as the author strives to read, interpret, and obey the Word of God to please the Lord while he will make effort to fulfill the new commandment "Love thy Neighbor as Thyself."

Chapter 15

Backlash From Black Supremacists

The author anticipates Backlash from Black Supremacists because he is not a supporter of their cause. The author detests issues of race based upon skin color, ethnicity, or any other issue connected to mistreatment of people. Black Supremist think everything that is white is from the devil. Black Supremist believe the so-called white man is the devil and stole, robbed, and killed to deceive, manipulate, and control everything around them. Black Supremist will do the opposite of the White Supremist and make everything black good and blame the so-called white man for everything that is wrong. Black Supremacy is wrong and evil just like White Supremacy is wrong and evil. Henceforth, the hatred towards those who are so-called white people is wrong and unfair to blame people today form what their ancestors may have or not have done.

Black Supremacy is different from White Supremacy because a person who is a Black Supremacist is not in political, social, or economic position to affect a so-called white person's life. They can say shocking or harmful things that may or may not be true. However, before classifying someone as a Black Supremacist one must differentiate between a person who is angry or hateful from a person who is seeking truth and facts.

There are so-called Black people who are seeking truth and facts labelled as a Black Supremacist because they find information that is contrary to the norms and beliefs of society. A person who is seeking the truth may discover that Joseph from the 12 Tribes of Israel own brothers did not recognize him and thought he was an Egyptian. The reason they did not recognize him because Egyptians and Hebrews had similar skin tones at that period. Egyptian people early in the bible had darker skin complexions prior to the Greek and Roman invasions. Egyptians were of darker complexion and looked like as so-called Black people and descendants of Noah's son Ham through Mizraim. Any person expressing their opinion or perception should have the right to say it without labeling. There are people seeking the truth and when they find information that is contrary to what the narrative of what White Supremacist wanted them to believe it causes problems. Nevertheless, let us delve into those who take truth seeking too far and combine it with anger and hate.

Most human beings become angry at various points of their lives, but most people do not let their anger turn into hatred and allow their lives to be guided by their hatred. It is reasonable for a human being to find out the truth about something they were previously deceived to believe and become angry. The author remembers believing in Santa Claus as a child and when he found out the truth that Santa Claus was not real, he became angry with his parents and wondered what else was not true. A feeling of betrayal and mistrust came into the relationship, but hatred never settled in, and the relationship was restorable. In the case of a person who becomes a Black Supremacist there is no restoration of a relationship and everything becomes the fault of their enemy. They believe all so-called white people are a devil, liar, racist, and hateful. A Black Supremacist tried to project their anger and distrust upon other so-called Black people so they can feel the same way they do. When a Black Supremacist learns of facts and truth from the past everything becomes one sided. Black Supremacist will only speak about the past greatness of kings, kingdoms, and accomplishments but will not disclose what led to their fall other than blaming the so-called white man. Black Supremacist know that they do not have the firepower or the numbers to overtake society. Unlike, a White Supremacist they cannot really affect they so-called white community except to make a little noise and disturb the peace because law enforcement already knows about them and is prepared for them.

The Nation of Islam in the United States and the Black Panther Party are not Hate Groups but classified as hate groups and were/are under the watchful eye of the (FBI) Federal Bureau of Investigations. The Nation of Islam is a religious organization that believes in Black economic empowerment and have helped individuals who were criminals or addicted to substances become clean and law-abiding citizens. There have been members of the Nation of Islam that have made comments over the years regarding so-called white people that display racist attitudes/slander towards so-called white people. Insomuch, individual members inside the Nation of Islam may qualify as a Black Supremacist, but the organization is not a Black Supremacist organization. Comments made by members and leaders reflect the individual/s perception but do not coincide with the goal of the religious organization. There may have been individuals in the Nation of Islam who had hatred towards so-called white people, but hatred was not part of the organization's objective. The Nation of Islam is a peaceful law-abiding religious group who does not go on the offensive regarding violence but will defend themselves if attacked. The Honorable Minister Louis Farrakhan became the leader of the Nation of Islam in 1975 after the passing of Elijah Muhammad in February of the same year. Likewise, the Black Panther Party is both different and like the Nation of Islam.

The Black Panther Party's goal was to help so-called Black neighborhoods to be safe and helped educate children and make sure people were fed. The Black Panther Party is not a religious organization, but their focus was to uplift the people in their neighborhood. Leaders and members of the Black Panther Party have made comments over the years regarding so-called white people perceived as a racist attitudes/slander towards so-called white people. Insomuch, there may be members inside the Black Panther Party that may qualify as a Black Supremacist, but the organization is not a Black Supremacist organization. The comments made by select members and leaders caused fear in the so-called white community, but the goal of the organization was to protect and improve their community and not to be violent towards anyone who was not showing violence against them. There may have been individuals that had hatred towards so-called white people but that was not part of the organization's objective. The Black Panther Party had a 10 Point Program that did focus on the government lack of concern for the so-called Black Community, and they called the government, military, and the police racist. [156] "We will protect ourselves from the force and violence of the racist police and the racist military by whatever means necessary." The Black Panther Party did not say they would seek to kill people but to protect themselves from any source that seeks to cause them harm. The party's demands in their 10 Point Program were controversial for conservative thinkers but understandable to progressive thinkers because they wanted a better life in their community. The author is not excusing or supporting any comments made by members of the Black Panther Party or The Nation of Islam. Any comments made by individuals should viewers assess the context by which they were. However, in both cases the organizations are not Black Supremacist as their goal consist of helping to improve and empower the so-called Black community and not to strike fear or cause harm to those who were not part of the community.

It is the hope of the author for Black Supremacists to turn off their anger and turn their hearts towards the Most- High God. Black Supremacist have called Jesus a "blue-eyed devil" created by the so-called white man and that Christianity is a white religion. There are beliefs and evidence that the Catholic Church intentionally commissioned artist to change the color of Jesus skin. The Catholic Church and changes could be a chapter of book to itself however there are often reasons that people feel the way they do. It is the author's hope that when the anger and blame released by the Black Supremacist

---

[156] BlackPost: https://www.blackpast.org/african-american-history/primary-documents-african-american-history/black-panther-party-ten-point-program-1966/

will repent and return to being a seeker of truth with love in their heart. When a person acquires information without consulting the spirit and having the spirit of God feelings of resentment can develop in any human. Hatred and holding grudges are an unbearable weight to carry that can only lead to destruction for the person carrying the excessive amount of weight. Therefore, the Black Supremacist must repent and turn their heart toward the Lord.

The author anticipates backlash from Black Supremacist because he believes in showing kindness towards all people and avoiding stereotyping people based upon preconceived information. If nine out of ten people fit a stereotype the author believes that it is still unfair to say all people fit a stereotype because one is an exception. The author also refuses to embrace someone else's rage or anger. Stating once again that a so-called Black person who is seeking truthful information and expresses what they have learned even if that information is upsetting to a different racial group of people that does not make that person a Black Supremacist. Disappointment and anger are natural reactions to finding out information that is different than what you previously believed. Disappointment and anger do not have to turn into hatred. The backlash from Black Supremacist could include criticism and hatred towards him for not agreeing with them. Therefore, it is the hope of the author that a backlash will not occur because the author considers himself a seeker of truth and wants justice for all people, but he will not participate in activities motivated by hatred.

Chapter 16
Backlash From Major Media

The author is not a public figure, and this book could fly under the radar of media attention. However, that could change if the findings of this book reach national attention the author could receive the backlash of scrutiny for reporting information against the believed norms. The media has a long history of portraying people of color in a negative light. When reporting crimes committed in the United States the media will report crimes of all races of people who commit them, but it is usually disproportionate to the negative for people of color. A common trend of the media is to make the public believe that most welfare recipients are people of color. For instance, a Google statistic says that 49% of African American people are on welfare, 36% of Hispanics, and 11% of Whites are on welfare. However, the reality is that Whites are the largest recipients of welfare at 37%, African Americans at 26%, and Hispanics 16% based upon the total population. The author uses the examples of welfare to show how truthful actual statistics are used to manipulate an agenda. Therefore, it would benefit the nation to read between the lines and think objectively and use "thinking outside of the box."

Earlier in this book the author discussed how Hollywood, television, magazines, radio, and now the internet can portray the agenda of the owners. One would have to ask who owns the media outlet and then discern what their motive is for the images they portrayed. The next question would be who benefits from the portrayals of people that a presented. Truthful and unbiased journalism does exist but the bottom line for most operations is to sell and make a profit. For one group of people to stay above they must keep another group of people down. The people who stay up are less than 1% of the population. It would be irresponsible and inaccurate to say that all so-called white people are up because there are more poor so-called white people than so called Black people regards to the total population. Today there are rich so-called African Americans. There are athletes and entertainers who are millionaires. Oprah Winfrey, Michael Jordan, and others have become billionaires since the turn of the 21st century. There are less known business professionals, medical professionals, and legal professionals of color who have become millionaires. Sports and entertainment are big business, and the media helps the profit machine continue. There are religious leaders who have become rich with their mega churches and television ministries seen throughout the world. It is not the author's place to judge which wealthy pastors are spreading the word of God as a calling or those who preach for money. However, there is a powerful backlash by the media that continues to happen.

The media loves a good scandal because scandals sell and make money. There have been famous people who have fallen by scandals of sex, drugs, alcohol, money, violence, and various crimes. The media does not discriminate and will report a scandal of a person of any race, ethnicity, or gender. However, it appears to the author that men are publicized more than women and so-called Black men more than white men. Harvey Weinstein a so-called white male and Bill Cosby a so-called Black male was both accused a sexual misconduct in Hollywood. Both incidents were reported by the media, but the Weinstein case seemed to disappear while Cosby was constantly in the news. Cosby served time in prison but later received an acquitted and released from prison, but his reputation and legacy will never be the same. Likewise, actor Robert Blake and actor/athlete O.J. Simpson both received acquittals of murdering their wife or former wife. Both men were popular in the 1970s, but most people do not know anything about Robert Blakes case, but most people will never forget O.J. Simpson's case as there was a racial divide on Mr. Simpson's guilt or innocence. In fairness to Weinstein and Blake neither one was as nationally popular as Cosby and Simpson, who were loved by millions of people in their prime by people of all races. Michael Jackson found innocent of molesting boys in his home but in the eyes of public opinion he is guilty. The author is not claiming innocence or guilt of any of the above-mentioned famous men but stating that accusations true or false stick with individuals regardless of what a court of law finds. Often, before a case goes before a judge or jury people are guilty until proven innocent but worse yet still guilty after proven innocent. Regardless of an acquittal or innocence by a jury the media can sway or raise doubt in public opinion and individuals' lives are never the same.

Public opinion influenced by the ownership of major media outlets. Women and minorities are not the owners or Chief Executive Officers (CEO) of major media therefore if that group feels threatened or they want to raise doubt about the research or the author they could do so. Popular and rich men like Bill Cosby, O.J. Simpson, and Michael Jackson were not able to overcome the stigma that the media placed upon them. The potential backlash by the media towards the author would not compare to what those three men endured. Nevertheless, a potential backlash does exist but hopefully but unlikely the media could embrace the findings by the author regarding leading all people including the lost and scattered tribes of Israel and Judah to Christ.

Chapter 17

Backlash From the Church of Jesus Christ of Latter-Day Saints

The author is prepared for a potential backlash from the Church of Jesus Christ of Latter-Day Saints, but he is hopeful that a backlash will not happen. The author converted to The Church of Jesus Christ of Latter-Day Saints in May of 1996 after attending Baptist Church during childhood and attending a Non-Denominational Church in young adulthood before marrying his wife who was already a member of the church. The author had questions and doubts about the Church of Jesus Christ of Latter-Day Saints but the genuine kindness he received from the members and leaders along with the fact that he could join the church without believing everything the church believes made him feel comfortable to join. He was an active member of the for years as he received the priesthood and held callings. The author had a personal falling out with the church and became disinterested with the church around 2014 and 2015. The author became inactive, rejected his calling, and attended other denominational churches. During the hiatus, the author enjoyed visiting different churches which included making periodical visits to The Church of Jesus Christ at periodically during the year. During the hiatus, members were still friendly towards the author, but treated the author as a dissenter and not treated as a member. The author never had his name removed from the membership roster.

Henceforth, the author never did or said anything critical of the church but when he abandoned his calling and became inactive, members of the church treated him differently.

The reason the author thinks there could be a backlash is because he wrote about things that may be embarrassing from the church's past regarding racism and polygamy. The author said unfavorable things about former church leadership including Joseph Smith and Brigham Young. However, the author's intent was not malicious but to tell the truth and explain his perspective of why he believes certain things happened.

The early Church of Jesus Christ of Latter-Day Saints had a history of excommunicating people who spoke against the desires of the church. The church had three witnesses that claimed they saw the plates the Book of Mormon who were, Oliver Cowdery, Martin Harris, and David Whitmer. Oliver Cowdery was a witness who also helped Joseph Smith scribe the Book of Mormon. Over time Oliver Cowdery disagreed with Joseph Smith on issues including being against polygamy. Oliver Cowdery issues led to excommunication from the church in 1838. The author was amazed that one of the witnesses and scribes to the Book of Mormon experienced excommunicated. Cowdery became a Methodist for a while but did return and join the church again in his later years and he never denounced the Book of Mormon. Martin Harris also left the church after a disagreement with Joseph Smith, and he did not have agreement with Brigham Young either. Martin Harris excommunicated in 1837. Harris like Cowdery made suspect comments but he never denounced the Book of Mormon, and he did return to the church in his later years. David Whitmer the third witness excommunicated from the church in 1837 and he decided to form his own branch of the Latter -Day Saint Church. Whitmer never followed the Utah branch but stayed as leader of his branch of saints but like the other witnesses he never denied the truthfulness of the Book of Mormon. Henceforth, the author speculates based upon research that around or before 1837 church leadership was branching away from the teachings of the

Book of Mormon and the three witnesses who confronted leadership became excommunicated because of their opposition.

The author believes that the church became carnal around 1837 and by reading the Doctrines and Covenants of the Church which is primarily declarations by Joseph Smith you can notice a shift in the revelations as they become more personal and less spiritual. Joseph Smith called out his wife and warned her that she should accept polygamy because it was the Lord's intent for man, and he used King David and Solomon as examples. That statement directly contradicted the Book of Mormon in The Book of Jacob which stated that David and Solomon were examples of what not to do of having many wives and that it was abominable, a man should have one wife and concubines they should have none. Each of the three witnesses only had one wife, which suggest to the author that each of them may have spoken against the practice of polygamy. The witness's documentation for being excommunicated for varied reasons other than polygamy opposition, but one must wonder if that has anything to do with it. Insomuch, there appears to be a long history of accusing members of being dissenters if they disagree with the leaders.

The author is unaware of what qualifies a member excommunicated other than various illegal crimes, adultery, physical abuse, substance abuse, or an ungodly lifestyle. The author is unaware if anyone excommunicated for differences with church leaders or telling truths that were not meant to be public. The author has come to the realization that it is better to have a church home and people who can help you or hold you accountable for teaching the gospel. The Church of Jesus Christ of Latter-Day Saints is full of members who strive hard to live and teach the gospel. The members are non-smokers, non-drinkers, and work hard and try to help other people. The church is family oriented and teaches how to be a better spouse, parent, and other roles. Henceforth, the author perceives that the positives of the church far outweigh the negatives of the church including its history.

The author believes the church has a solid foundation that is valuable to the kingdom of heaven. The author has seen the church have a good record of service towards helping their fellow man. Research by the author appears to validate the Book of Mormon not as equal to the bible but as another Testament of Jesus Christ. The Book of Mormon tells of a family from the lineage of Joseph of the 12 Tribes of Israel to escape the capture and wrath of King Nebuchadnezzar of Babylon which period coincides with the Bible, World History, and historical origins of Native Americans in South America. Even though the author accepts the connection between the Bible and the Book of Mormon he only accepts it as face value of what the church says as another testament of Jesus Christ. The author believes the bible teaches salvation, but he loves to increase his knowledge by reading other books such as The Book of Enoch, The Book of Jasher, The Book of Jubilees, other Apocrypha Books, as well as The Book of Mormon. Members in the church might find the author's outlook towards the Book of Mormon irritating because they believe the Book of Mormon has less errors and is more important than the bible. Regardless, of the differences between the author's perspective of the church's perspective the author believes The Book of Mormon has merit where he used to doubt its validity upon a falling out with the church. Furthermore, the author believes the founder of The Church of Jesus Christ of Latter-Day Saints Joseph Smith did see a vision and have revelations which makes him a prophet of God. Joseph Smith was a young man who was seeking to learn more about God and the bible. The Book of James inspired Joseph Smith. [157] "If any of you lack wisdom, let him ask of God, that giveth to all men liberally, and upbraideth not; and it shall be given him." At about 14 years old he was seeking a church to join when he had a vision. Joseph Smith had limited education and the author doubts that he could fake a story and create a book that would convince thousands of people. Therefore, the author accepts Joseph Smith's history and believes that the early church members were earnestly seeking to serve the savior.

---

[157] James 1:5 (KJV)

The author does not seek to damage or disrespect The Church of Jesus Christ of Latter- Day Saints. He is referencing the facts as he learned them and adding his perspective. The bible never stated that a man or prophet of God could not make a mistake or use poor judgment if caught up in the flesh. The author shared his perspective that he believed that the first two presidents made statements and decisions based upon their flesh regarding polygamy and Black men in the priesthood. However, the author believes their spiritual inspirations and leadership was effective and impactful and inspired members to seek salvation through Jesus Christ.

The Church of Jesus Christ has grown and number and matured in leadership since its early days. The mature statement is not a put down to the early church because all people hopefully mature over the years and share their wisdom to help the next generation. The author respects the leadership of the church (new and old) and does not consider himself a prophet or an apostle, meaning that he recognizes that he does not maintain all the keys of priesthood authority. Priesthood should be respected and revered as well as positions of authority. The author genuinely believes that the members of The Church of Jesus Christ of Latter-Day Saints are Christians and a true church. The author does not believe the Church of Jesus Christ of Latter-Day Saints is the only true church as some members state in their personal testimonies. The author believes what the Book of Mormon says that there are two churches one of God and the other of the devil. Therefore, any church that is teaching things that are not supported by the bible is either teaching in error or teaching doctrines of devils.

Prior to 1978 the church was in error of teaching things not supported by the bible. That is why the author says there is a difference between a Mormon and a Latter Day Saint. Mormons believe and teach things not supported by the bible because of their blind confidence in leadership. This is why the church was classified as a cult by some Christians. Some of the author's favorite preachers to watch on YouTube Darby, Jennings, MacAuthur, Parr, Kim, and few others have publicly classified the church as a cult or have false doctrine. Nevertheless, the author feels that he was instructed to reread and examine the Book of Mormon which led to his discoveries and forgiving the church of things they avoided about church history.

The church is more diverse than it ever has been and more accepting of racial and cultural differences. The hope of the author consists of the leadership of The Church of Jesus Christ of Latter-Day Saints will read this book, ponder the findings, pray about it, seek direction about what to do with the information, accept the findings, and support the author's findings as beginning to usher in a new era of the church to proclaim and identify the lost and scattered Tribes of Israel and Judah to teach the gospel of Jesus Christ. The author would welcome the opportunity to travel and teach his findings.

Part Seven
Teaching the Gospel

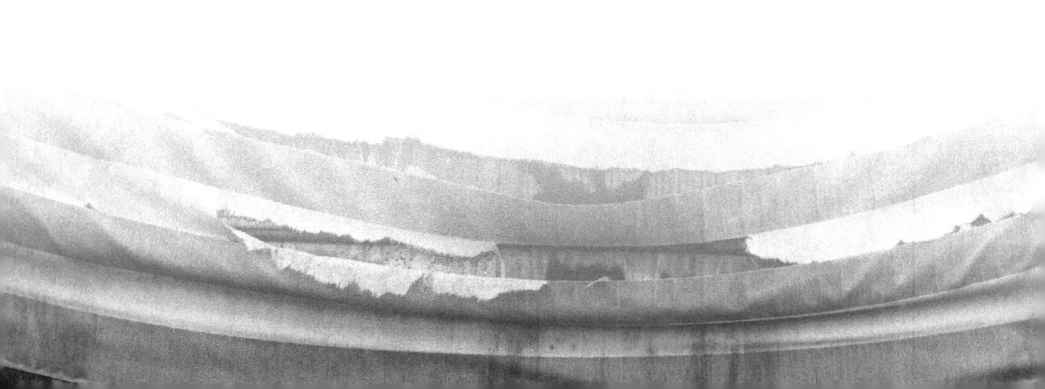

CHAPTER 18

THE GOSPEL OF JESUS CHRIST

The Gospel of Jesus Christ is the most important thing in a true believer's life. A true believer is genuinely concerned about their eternal life and what they need to do to live with the Lord in Heaven. There are also casual and convenient believers who are not as attentive towards living the Gospel of Jesus Christ. For people who may be serious about their salvation their motivation is to avoid going to Hell. Unfortunately, casual, or convenient believers think there is a middle ground and try to keep one foot in the world by doing sinful things to gratify their flesh and have the other foot in the church to be able to have connections with God so they can go to Heaven and avoid Hell. The problem is that the middle ground does not exist, and we must choose who we are going to serve. [158] "No servant can serve two masters: for either he will hate the one and love the other; or else he will hold to the one and despise the other. Ye cannot serve God and mammon. Since humankind is both flesh and spirit there is a constant battle between them." [159] "For the flesh lusteth against the Spirit, and the Spirit against the flesh: and these are contrary the one to the other: so that ye cannot do the things that ye would." Therefore, those who choose to serve the Lord must do so by obeying the spirit over the flesh.

Humankind focuses on the flesh and worldly desires while

---

[158] Luke 16:13 (KJV)
[159] Galatians 5:17 (KJV)

God is concerned with our spiritual well-being. It is humankind that places importance on race, ethnicity, socioeconomic status, gender, education, and other statuses that separates and elevates one classification of people over another. The bible tells us that God is not a respecter of persons therefore we should not be respecter of people either. The color of a person's skin is insignificant to God but with humankind it became important to individuals. A person's bloodline is insignificant to a degree because most people have a mixed bloodline including our savior Jesus Christ according to the books of Matthew and Luke in the bible. The Lord promised to redeem the lost and scattered tribes of people who do not know or understand who they are to God. The world likes to call them the chosen people. However, if a person from a chosen bloodline still rejects Christ, they will have the same fate as others who reject Christ and were not from a certain bloodline.

While Jesus was on earth, He instructed his disciples to teach the gospel and spread it across the earth. Jesus also commissioned his greatest earthly adversary in Saul who became Paul after the Lord confronted him. Paul became the greatest crusader for the gospel and credited with writing half of the New Testament. The Apostle Paul's ministry primarily consisted of preaching and teaching the gentiles. The gentiles of the day were in modern terms of European descent. The Apostle Paul a Jew from the Tribe of Benjamin of the 12 Tribes of Israel. Nevertheless. Paul lived in Rome before his conversion to Christ and he was very skilled in his leadership and communication with the gentiles.

The author does not think it was an accident that Paul preached the Gospel of Jesus Christ to the gentiles because they had the means or would develop the technology in the future to spread the gospel across the world. In modern society gentiles have sent Christian missionaries to so-called Third World Countries and remote locations on the planet preaching the gospel. Bible colleges, television, radio, print media, and other items have built to preach the Gospel of Jesus Christ across the world. The wise gentiles recognized their need for a savior and accepted the responsibility of teaching and spreading the gospel. The important thing that happened as the gospel spread across the globe that those who received the gospel began to spread the gospel. Unfortunately, the unwise gentiles work against Christ, and will use Christ as a mean to make profit, pervert the Word of God, and lead people astray. The bible gives harsh warnings to those who lead people away from Christ regardless of the color of their skin. Insomuch, the Old Testament, New Testament, Apocrypha Books, and The Book of Mormon paint a gloomy picture for anyone who opposes the Will of God in the time of judgment.

There are prophecies in the Old Testament that refer to what people call the "Last Days" when Christ returns to earth to roam as King of Kings and Lord of Lords. Identifying the Historic Lost and Scattered Tribes of Israel and Judah is important when it comes to knowing who the bible is talking about. The bible will become scary for those who are living in opposition to the will of God and Gospel of Jesus Christ. The Gospel of Jesus Christ is not all about prosperity of wealth and health but includes warnings of doom and gloom for non-believers. Part of the doom and gloom is learning that the so-called "Last Day" is not the end, but it is transitional day. The author's wife discovered this during their bible study. Last Day and The Resurrection Day are two different things. Every person's last day is the day they die and leave this physical realm. The Resurrection Day is the day Christ returns to earth and calls up those who lived for Him during their time on earth in the first resurrection. Those who did not live for Christ during their time on earth will call up later in the second resurrection which may be affectionately known as Judgement Day. However, judgment must take place when we die to identify who ends up in either the first or second resurrection spoken of in the Book of Revelations Chapter 20. The world will continue with Jesus' reigning in both physical and spiritual realms. Unfortunately, people will choose not to accept the gift of salvation. Insomuch, they cannot receive grace and mercy in the physical realm, or have their transgressions forgiven and the blood of Christ erase their sins because they rejected Jesus Christ as their Lord and Savior.

Jesus bled, suffered, and died on the cross so that all men's salvation. He rose from the grave three days later as He said He would. However, there is one stipulation that they must accept Him as their Lord and Savior. It appears so people want to avoid saying that Jesus Christ is their Lord and Savior and try to find alternative routes to heaven when there are not any alternative routes to heaven. [160] "Whosoever therefore shall confess me before men, him will I confess also before my Father which is in heaven." [161] "But whosoever shall deny me before men, him will I also deny before my Father which is in heaven." The bible is clear that the road to heaven and the Father goes through Jesus. While Jesus was on earth, He performed miracles such as giving sight to the blind, healing the sick, casting out demons, restoring the dead, walking on water, and turning water into wine so people would believe that He was who He said that he was. People converted and believed during Christ on earth, but still resisted accepting Jesus. Insomuch, if people who were there during the time Jesus was performing miracles on earth still chose not to accept Him, how much more difficult will it be for those people who never seen Him to believe in Him.

The Gospel of Jesus Christ is a simple thing for people who are in tune with their spiritual side. However, for people who do not look beyond the physical realm it does not make sense. The physical world does not deny that Jesus existed, but they deny who He is and why He came. The physical world rejects the bible and what it says therefore putting people at risk for missing the Gospel of Jesus Christ. Fortunately, people have a spiritual side and when they hear the truth of the Gospel of Jesus Christ, they can decide for themselves if they want to live by the instructions the Word of God gives humankind. Believers appointed to be ministers and missionaries of the Gospel of Jesus Christ in our everyday lives that people may understand something clearly at last of God within us. Insomuch, the light that shows through us in this shadowy world may spark an interest of those living in darkness and starving for spiritual nourishment through the Gospel of Jesus Christ.

---

[160] Matthew 10:32 (KJV)
[161] Matthew 10:33 (KJV)

Chapter 19

How The Author's Theory Connects to the Gospel of Jesus Christ

The author's theory is rooted in the Gospel of Jesus Christ. The goal consists of introducing the gospel to people who will receive it that they may choose to have a relationship with Jesus Christ and receive eternal life through Him. The author believes that individual segments of people do not believe that the Gospel of Jesus Christ applies to them primarily because of the condition of their lives, personal sin, environment, family structure, mistreatment, and other elements that may be oppressive. The author wants to make it clear that his secondary focus is saving our country from ourselves not the so-called black and white issue. There are so-called good people of all races and ethnicities and there are so-called bad people in each as well. The main goal is to help people receive the Gospel of Jesus Christ and take upon His righteousness and save souls through Him. Unfortunately, masses of people are still asleep regarding their historic identity and do not know their own genealogical historic origin because their information is hidden from them to their disadvantage.

The author is not claiming to be the first person to identify the historic lost and scattered tribes of Israel and Judah. Insomuch, the author learned from those who documented and shared information before him regarding the identification of the lost and scattered. Even though the author claims that so-called Black people in the Americas are part of the lost and scattered tribes of Judah and Israel he is also claiming that not all so-called Black people are part of the lost and scattered tribes. Various authors such as Windsor" From Babylon to Timbuktu" provided information of how Israel scattered across the globe including a large migration to Africa. Van Sertima "They Came Before Columbus" provided information about how African sailors came to the Americas. Dalton Jr, "Hebrews to Negros" was a well-researched book that provided various information regarding the author's topic. Smith, E. "View of the Hebrews" provided information of the Native Americans in America had Hebrew roots. Israel, "Into Egypt Again with Ships" connected the Atlantic Slave Trade to Deuteronomy Chapter 28", and the "Book of Mormon" connected the Tribes of Israel to Native Americans to the American Continents. The previous authors mentioned along with multiple other sources helped shape or support the author's theory. Likewise, the author utilized the scriptures, history, documents, maps, charts, and concepts from other theorist to formulate his own theory and connection to the bible.

Regardless, of all the outside research conducted by the author the bible was the most essential element into formulating his theory. The story in the Book of Genesis where the brothers of Joseph of the 12 Tribes of Israel not recognizing their brother had a tremendous impact upon the author developing his theory. The descendants of Israel were from Noah's son Shem and the descendants of Egypt was through Noah's son Ham. The author discovered through research of others that Shem and Ham must have had similar features which included dark skin. However, the descendants of Ham were not fearing the God of Shem which became the God of Abraham, Isaac, and Jacob. Nevertheless, all people on earth are descendants of Noah and his three sons, regardless of genealogical lineage any person can accept The Gospel of Jesus Christ.

The author highly encourages people to read and re-read the bible for themselves. When people read the bible, they will have distinct levels of understanding. Seasoned Christians who have read the bible may read one of their familiar passages and get a different understanding or revelation at a particular time and season. The author used to skip over genealogy in the bible until one day over 10 years ago. When they author began seeing who begot who and what family lineage people came from, he began to see the bible in a different light. However, based upon the images engraved in his mind from artwork, books, magazines, television, and the movies he envisioned everyone in the bible having European features and so-called white skin. The idea that anyone in the bible besides the Ethiopians being so-called Black people did not exist. In movies Hollywood always portrayed people in power positions as so-called white males. Nimrod the son of Cush the son of Ham within whom credited for populating the darker skinned people in Africa portrayed as a so-called white male because of his power position and influence over the masses. A so-called white male actor always portrays Pharoah the King of Egypt even though the cave paintings depicting the leaders of Egyptians range from brown to copper colored skin people. Insomuch, the author is not concerned with the actual skin color people as is his concern for the discrepancy between historical and archeological information verses the perception painted by Hollywood.

The so-called white physical appearance of people known as Jewish people today are assumed as how the biblical Jewish people looked in the past. The author never questioned the perception and assumption given to him until over 10 years ago. The author heard of people saying that Jesus was so-called black before, but the idea went in one ear and out of the other because in the author's mind nothing black could be good and Jesus was good. The good so-called Black people had to act like the good so-called white people to be acceptable in society. Henceforth, a good so-called Black person could be in the fields of entertainment, sports, education, medicine, law, or so-called blue-collar laborer if they separated themselves from a stereotypical so-called Black person.

The reason the author uses the term so-called throughout the book consists of his dislikes for stereotyping people and placing labels upon individuals. Society has the tendency to dismiss or belittle anything or anyone they disagree with or do not understand. A small percentage of society is cruel to other people who are different from themselves, and they understand the negative impact cruelty can have upon a person. The best way to overcome a negative impact placed upon a person is to fill that person with truth and love. Therefore, the author believes that if we provide people with truth and give them the love of the Lord.

The author has collaborated with people who have felt less than others because they do not know their personal history. So-called African Americans believe their roots trace them back to slavery and Africa. However, they do not know the history of their family prior to the Atlantic Slave Trade. Often so-called African American families cannot trace their genealogy beyond their grandparents. Foster children may know their birth families, but do not know anything about their biological families. The so-called African Americans lack biological information more than other races and ethnicities but foster children of all races and ethnicities may suffer from lack of identity. Henceforth, the author's goal is to provide information to people who are lacking identity and let them know their history has biblical roots. All people have biblical roots, and all people have a mixed lineage. However, most importantly is our spiritual connection through Christ which is the only lineage that really matters. Therefore, the author hopes to inform people that the bible is for everyone, and Jesus Christ can save the soul of anyone who accepts him.

The bible uses an example of people being like branches to a tree. [162] "For if thou wert cut out of the olive tree which is wild by nature, and wert grafted contrary to nature into a good olive tree: how much more shall these, which be the natural branches, grafted into their own olive tree?" A wild olive tree branch represents Gentiles, Africans, Asian, Hispanic, or anyone who was not through the line of Shem through Abraham, Isaac, and Jacob that decides to accept Jesus Christ as Lord and Savior. They will graft into the

---

[162] Romans 11:24 (KJV)

good Olive Tree which is the body of Christ. Likewise, the natural olive branches are the people who are of the lost and scattered tribes of Israel and Judah who disconnected and need to graft back in. Insomuch, the bible says that all have sinned and fall short of the glory of God therefore regardless of, if a branch (person) is wild or natural they disconnect from the tree and need grafting to the good tree (body of Christ).

Chapter 20

How to Teach the Gospel to the Lost and Scattered

Teaching the gospel to the lost and scattered tribes of Israel and Judah should not be any different than teaching the gospel to anyone who is ready to receive the gospel. Various people of the lost and scattered tribes of Israel and Judah have already received the Gospel of Jesus Christ without knowing who the lost and scattered tribes of Israel and Judah are. Those who have already received the Gospel of Jesus Christ either did not know or care if they were part of the lost and scattered tribes because they accepted Jesus Christ as their Lord and Savior. Truthfully, the Gospel of Jesus Christ is the "Good News," and the message of Christ as our Savior is enough without knowing one's physical genealogy.

Various people from different races, nationalities, and ethnicities suffer emotionally and psychologically disconnected from their family roots. So-called Black people suffer from the disconnection of their family roots disproportionately due to the historical disruption of the family unit. There is controversial documentation "Willie Lynch Letter" used as evidence to explain the phenomenon of the numbers of so-called Black people from mother as head of the household families, poverty rates, incarceration rates, abortion rates, and other factors today the displays them in a negative light. Each area mentioned improves if the so-called Black Community would repent and live by the standards of the bible while accepting

Jesus Christ as their Lord and Savior. The government, politicians, educators, and so forth cannot fix the problems in the so-called Black Community or overcome the self-managing effects of former slaves taught by the controversial "Willie Lynch Letter and Making a Slave." Henceforth, the information the author learned about lead him to further evaluation of the so-called Black Community.

The discovery of information can lead any investigator down a path that may not be prosperous. The author discovered that the letter "J" did not exist during Jesus' time on earth and that the apostles given English names in translation to the Greek, Hebrew, and Arabic scriptures. The author discovered that Pope Alexander VI commissioned Leonardo Da Vinci to paint Jesus to appear European. Leonardo used the Pope's son Cesare Borgia as his model to be Jesus who it is rumored that Da Vinci and Borgia were gay lovers. The author discovered other information about the Catholic Church that took his focus off spiritual matters and placed them on conspiracy theories. Therefore, the additional information created more questions than answers for the author.

The question/s becomes how people rejected the Gospel of Jesus Christ because they did not believe that the gospel pertained to them? How did people grow up thinking a curse was upon them and nothing good could happen for them? How people grew up thinking that God does not love them or that God does not exist because I do not think a loving God would allow the terrible things happen to me? People of all races and ethnicities could have the same questions and doubts as mentioned in the previous sentences. However, there are also a small segment of people that believe that Christianity is a so-called white man's religion created to keep the so-called Black man down. Henceforth, the author has always believed Christianity is for all people but thinks he can help share information to bring the good news of the gospel to all people.

The author's experience in ministry to this point has been collaborating with people who are downtrodden of all colors. The author currently holds weekly bible studies at a homeless shelter. Previously he participated and alternated lead teaching bible study in a men's jail ministry called "Forgotten Man Ministry" when he lived in Michigan. The author has also previously shared the Word of God in a Nursing Home, hospital, and private homes of individuals temporarily shut in. Outside of teaching the downtrodden the author and his wife currently hold weekly bible study on a zoom meet which is open to anyone who wants to join called "Read it 4 Yourself Ministries". The author and his wife also attend local church service on Sundays. The author has found that people are hungry for the Word of God, but more people seem disinterested. However, for those people who are hungry for the word most have general working knowledge of the bible at the milk level but very few are at the meat level of the gospel.

The bible mentioned about how God loves Jacob/Israel and hates Esau/Edom. There is small segment of people who believe Israel and Edom is a so-called black and white issue. The author believes that Israel and Edom are a spiritual issue between those who accept The Gospel of Jesus Christ and those who accept the ways of the world without Christ. Anyone who is so-called black, brown, red, yellow, or white can either accept or reject the gospel. Likewise, the historic lost and scattered tribes of Israel and Judah today will include a multitude of variations of skin tones and people of various ethnicities because of the scattering.

Identifying the historic lost and scattered tribes of Israel and Judah is a spiritual meat level teaching message. It would not be productive to approach so-called Black people in the Americas and tell them you are part of the lost and scattered tribes of Israel and Judah. The first reason it would be unproductive is that it cannot be prove concretely because we did not live in those times but theoretically there is an argument because of available information. The bloodlines of Ham and Shem have been thoroughly intermingled along with descendants of Japheth that it does not make sense to create a conflict about the subject. Secondly, so-called Black people have either rejected the possibility of being a descendant of Shem or use the information they are a descendant of Shem and become prideful by thinking they are the chosen people, and their flaws and sins overlooked without changing their lifestyle to serve God. Henceforth, the information is serious spiritual meat and not spiritual milk that would choke so-called Black people, or any Christian not seasoned in the Word.

The author has found that you cannot give spiritual meat to baby Christians because people need background knowledge and a firm foundation of the scriptures first. Baby Christians will like the flavor of the spiritual meat but, it will choke them which will scare them from the spiritual meat meaning that it can hinder their spiritual development. The author did not come to this conclusion until after starting to author this book. Prior to researching and authoring this book the author believed he could tell individuals that you are of the lost and scattered tribes of Judah and Israel without problems. There has already been groups of people who have stated that so-called Black people are the true Hebrew Israelites. They have awakened people to search for truth but unfortunately, they are in danger of repeating the mistakes of the past by falling into pride about their newfound knowledge. God said that He resist the proud in the bible. The author witnessed so-called Black individuals overcome by the pride of knowledge. Therefore, the author concludes that individuals who read the bible for themselves, follow the bible instructions, and accept Jesus Christ as Lord and Savior receive salvation. Likewise, those who do not read the scriptures for themselves, disregard biblical instructions, and reject The Gospel of Jesus Christ have also rejected their eternal inheritance and will inherit the fate of spiritual Edom, Satan, and Satan's followers regardless of their individual bloodline.

This book did speak about the author's belief that so-called African Americans are part of the people from the historic lost and scattered and lost tribes of Israel and Judah. It is not conclusive that all so-called African Americans have Hebrew origins through the father's lineage. The bible stated that the tribes were scattered to the four corners of the earth, therefore the islands in the Caribbean, South America, Asia, Africa, Australia, Pacific Islanders, as well as islands nations in the Indian Ocean may all include remnants of the scattered tribes who do not know their origin. The author hopes that the information provided in this book is a starting point to increase respect and self-esteem of all people. All people of all races and ethnicities can receive Christ and be saved. The author's concern is individual American people are turning away from the scriptures and serving Satan most unknowingly. Insomuch, if a person does not purposely choose Jesus Christ, they are inadvertently serving themselves and indirectly serving Satan.

America can be great if we stop trying to be superior to others. Nobody has a pure bloodline including Jesus Christ as shown in Matthew Chapter One, and we are all related if we go back far enough to the family of Noah. All people on earth may have Semitic, Japhetic, and Hamitic blood. Through obedience to the Lord, America can reverse any curse that came from disobedience to the Word of God. Therefore, by accepting the truth, repenting, forgiving, being forgiven, and following the Lord we can save America.

Bibliography

Bible Gateway. Bible Gateway.com. Grand Rapids. 2021.

Bible Timelines and Charts. Bible Timeline Chart With World History: Austin. 2022 https://amazingbibletimeline.com/?creative&device=c&placement&utm_agid&utm_campaign=Pmax-StarterPPC&utm_matchtype&utm_medium=cpc&utm_source=google&utm_term

BlackPast, B. The Black Panther Party Ten-Point Program. 1966. July 2022. https://www.blackpast.org/african-american-history/primary-documents-african-american-history/black-panther-party-ten-point-program-1966/

Bradt, Steve. One Drop Rule Persist. 2010. May 2022. The Harvard Gazette. https://news.harvard.edu/gazette/story/2010/12/one-drop-rule-persists/

Calloway, Dane. Tracing Your Family's Genealogical Historical History By Records. I'm Just Her to Make You Think. 2016.

Cooper, Kenneth. For African-Americans Determining Native American Ancestry Often a Challenge. Diverse: Issues in Higher Education. 2014. 2021 https://diverseeducation.com/article/68068

Covenant Christian Coalition. The Complete Apocrypha. Covenant Press. 2018.

Dalton Jr, Ronald. Hebrews to Negroes: Wake Up Black America United States of America: G Publishing LLC, 2014

Dauid, Huldah. Hidden in Plain Sight: The Revelations of the Sons of Yah. California: 2019

Fortson, Dante. Hiding the Hebrews: Did America Kidnap the Lost Tribes of Israel? South Carolina: Fortson, 2019.

Israel, Elisha J. Into Egypt Again with Ships: A Message to the Forgotten Israelites. United States of America: 2008

James, Frank. Helen Thomas Retires After Anti-Israeli Jew Remarks. The Two-Way. 2010, 2020. https://www.npr.org/sections/thetwoway/2010/06/Helen Thomas 'Retires'After Anti-Israeli Jew Remarks: The Two-Way: NPR

Johnson, John L. The Black Biblical Heritage: Four Thousand Years of Biblical Black Heritage. Nashville: Winston-Derek Publishers. 1993

Lamb, Andrew. Faith: Why Mormons No Longer Want to be Called Mormons. Kamloops This Week. May 29, 2019. May 2022. https://www.kamloopsthisweek.com/community/faith-why-mormons-no-longer-want-to-be-called-mormons-4440040.

Lawrence-Harper, Derek. The Origins of SelFLESHness: Based on the Scriptures, Ohio: Empowerment Zone Publishing, 2020

Lynch, Willie. The Willie Lynch Letter: The Making of a Slave. 1712.

McConkie, Bruce. Mormon Doctrine, 1966

Meme. 2nd President of Egypt Gamel Abdel Nasser. Television Broadcast. 1952 2021. https://me.me./i2nd-president-of-egypt-gamel-abdel-nasser-You-jews-will-15406580.

Mendenhall, George E. Ancient Israel's Faith and History: An Introduction to the Bible in Context. Louisville: Westminster John Knox Press, 2001

Norton, Kimberly. Black People are Indigenous to the Americas: Research MaterialFor the Inquisitive. 2016

Perkins, Marvin & Gray, Darius. Blacks in the Scriptures. Santa Clara CA. DVD www.BLACKSintheSCRIPTURES.com. 2007

Pew Research Center. Pew Research. 2021.2021. www.pewresearch.org

Prophet, Elizabeth Clare. Fallen Angels and the Origins of Evil. Montana: Summit University Press. 2000.

Shalev, Chemi. The Mystery of the Lost Jewish Colony and the Myth of the Lost Hebrew-Indian Tribes. Haaretz. 2016. 2021 https://www.haaretz.com/world-news/americas/.premium-the-mystery-of-the-lost-jewish-colony-and-hebrew-indian-tribe-1.5449822

Smith, Ethan. View of the Hebrews or The Ten Lost Tribes of Israel in North America. Adansonia Press. 1823, 2018

Smith, Joseph F. The Way to Perfection. The Church of Jesus Christ of Latter-Day Saints. (1984)

The Church of Jesus Christ of Latter-Day Saints. All are Alike Unto God. Official Declaration 2. 1978. 2022. https://www.churchofjesuschrist.org/study/scriptures/dc-testament/od/2?lang=eng

The Church of Jesus Christ of Latter-Day Saints. "Mormon" is Out: Church Releases Statement of How to Refer to the Organization. August 2019. June 2022. https://www.churchofjesuschrist.org/church/news/mormon-is-out-church-releases-statement-on-how-to-refer-to-the-organization?lang=eng

The Church of Jesus Christ of Latter-Day Saints. Journal of Discourses. Digital Collections BYU Library. 2022 https://contentdm.lib.byu.edu/digital/collection/JournalOfDiscourses3/id/9599/

The Church of Jesus Christ of Latter-Day Saints. The Book of Mormon Another Testament of Jesus Christ. Salt Lake City: 1830, 1981

The Church of Jesus Christ of Latter-Day Saints. The Articles of Faith. The Pearl of Great Price. 1851.

U.S. Department of State. Defining Anti-Semitism. 2021. https://www.state.gov/defining-anti-semitism/

V, Delta. The Letter "J" was not Invented Until the 1500's, So How was there a Jesus or John or Jacob or Jonah or Joseph or Jude in the Bible? Believers vs. Non-Believers. August 28, 2015. August 2020. https://believervsnonbelievers.wordpress.com/2015/04/28/the-letter-j-was-not-invented-until-the-1500s-so-how-was-there-a-jesus-or-john-or-jacob-or-jonah-or-joseph-or-jude-in-the-bible/

Van Sertima, Ivan. They Came Before Columbus: The African Presence in Ancient America. New York: 1976, 2003

Windsor, Rudolph. From Babylon to Timbuktu: A History of Ancient Black Races Including the Black Hebrews. Philadelphia: Windsor Golden Series, 1969, 2020.

Woodson, Carter G. The Mis-Education of the Negro. Oshun Publishing. 1933, 1999.

Yashar'el, Beneyah. Esau-Rome The Hidden Identity of the Man of Sin. Bahamas: Yashar'el, 2020

Young, Margeret & Gray, Darius. Standing on the Promises: Book 1 One More River To Cross. Salt Lake City: Bookcraft. 2000.

Zondervan, Zondervan Compact Bible Dictionary. Grand Rapids, Zondervan Academic, 1967, 1993

ARTWORK BY THE AUTHOR

Dr. Derek Lawrence-Harper "The Minister Artist" is a minister, artist, author, and educator. Much of his artwork is either telling a story or teaching a lesson. Biblical themes, spiritual references, and social issues are common in his artwork. The artist loved cartoons and comics as a child which reflects in his adult artistic style. The artist has created paintings in various artistic styles, but he is most enthusiastic about using characters in a muralist style to tell a story. Four of his artworks are displayed on the following pages.

ARTWORK BY
THE AUTHOR

Artwork by Dr. Derek Lawrence-Harper "The Minister Artist"

Nine Eleven 24x 36 painting created in 2002. This artwork depicts how a country can drop any differences and come together as a nation. This artwork was featured in the Midland Daily News (MI) in 2002 in recognition of the one-year anniversary of the tragic day.

Children at Play 46x47 painting inspired by

Zechariah 8:5: And the streets of the city shall be full of boys and girls playing in the streets thereof.

This painting represents modern activities such as basketball, soccer, baseball, football, jump rope, beach volleyball, swimming, and a father and young son rolling the ball to each other.

Peaceful fun and competition. Unity and love.

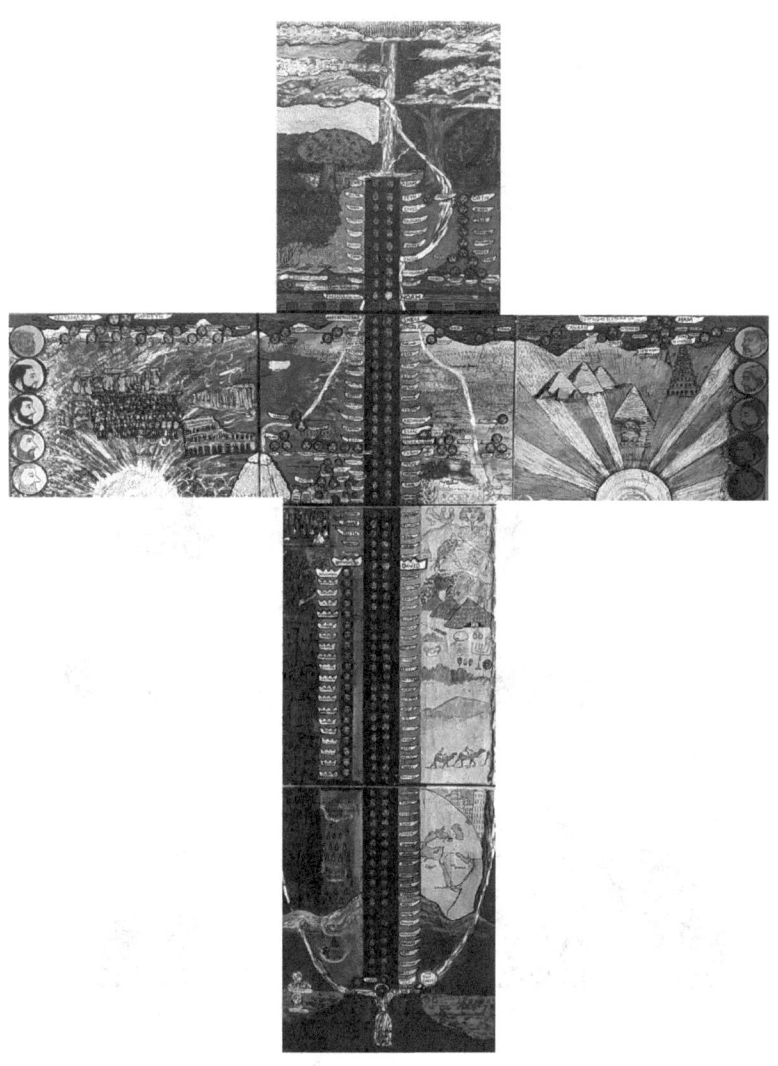

Adam to Jesus 72x60 painting.

This painting took extensive research to find the names of the wives as well as the men mentioned in the Genealogy of Jesus mentioned in The Book of Luke Chapter 3. The Book of Jubilees, Geni, and other Genealogical sites were used to find the female names.

Note the research for the female names was conducted prior to 2016. The wives of Noah's sons were sisters on this site. As of 2022 the wives of Noah's sons have changed and are no longer shown related. Things that make you wonder??

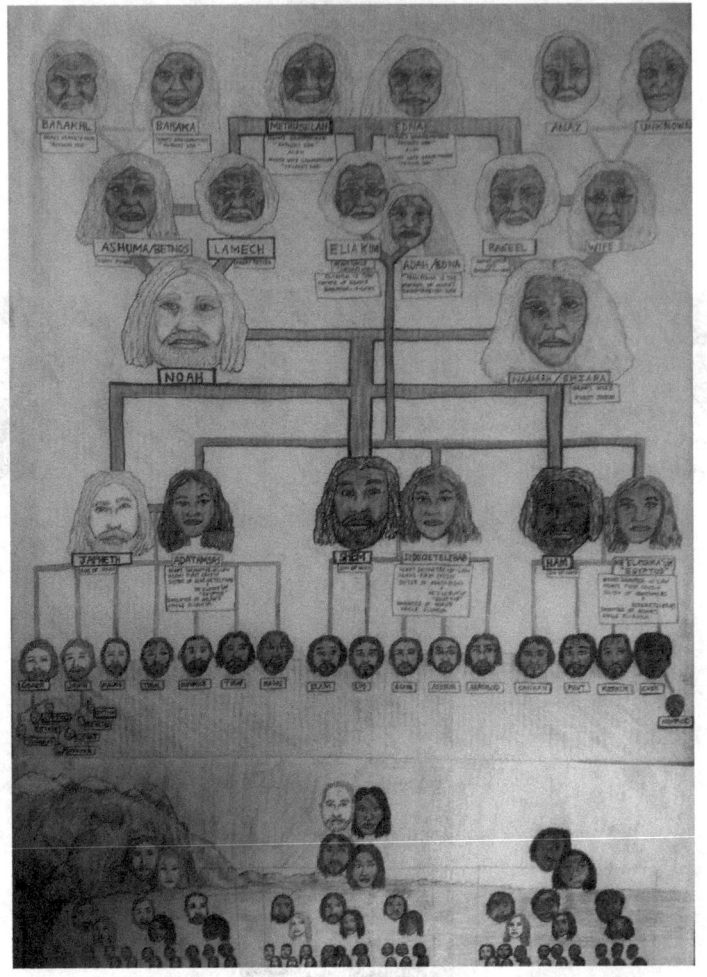

Noah's Genealogy. 37x26 Color Pencil Drawing with ink.

1. The top row of this drawing depicts Noah and his wife's grandparents.
2. The second row depicts Noah and his wife's parents.
3. The third row depicts Noah and his wife.
4. The Book of Enoch 105: 1-3 refers to Noah's skin being white as snow and scaring his father Lamech because he looked different from other people.
5. The fourth row depicts Noah's three sons and their wives who were sisters.
6. The fifth row depicts the grandchildren. Genesis 10.

The last section depicts how different skin tones and races developed through intermarriage and producing children.

"**The Origins of SelFLESHness**: Based upon the Scriptures" Is the first book written by "The Minister Artist" now Dr. Derek Lawrence-Harper.

The book is full of information about the sins of selfishness and the sins of the flesh and where it began. The book also contains some interesting theories about where we came from in the bible and other sources to who we have become today. This book also includes our need for salvation through Jesus Christ.